**Praise for**

"[*Words at Work*] provides a wealth of advice—including specific exercises—to prompt business writers to write well. Unlike most business-writing courses and books that are dry and dull, McDaniel's work is a breezy, well-written how-to guide, nicely held together with stories of her experiences. The author is unafraid to illustrate some of her lessons with personal challenges and failures, which may be the best teacher. ... Thankfully, McDaniel presents all of the material in the book clearly, concisely, and with a healthy dose of encouragement based on the optimistic belief that 'everyone can learn to write well' and that 'bad writers just stopped too soon.'...The book's readability is proof positive that the author's counsel is sound. A timely manual that business people at any level will find useful."
—Kirkus Discoveries Review

"Using stories from her own journey as a writer and coach, Lynda gently nudges even the most insecure writers to push aside their fears and trust their ability to write well. You'll go back to *Words at Work* again and again for inspiration and practical advice."
—Virginia McCullough, author of numerous books
www.virginiamccullough.com

"*Words at Work* is a short storybook full of true tales from the writing life of successful publicist and writing coach. Lynda introduces us to the key lessons anyone needs to effectively connect with others through words on paper and screen. Along the way she introduces us to her mentors, and by doing so makes them our own, and in the process, her book becomes a gift."
—Dan Kennedy, Results That Matter
www.resultsthatmatter.com, Seattle, Wash.

*continued...*

"Good writing skills are a solid predictor of career success and in this excellent and engaging reference, McDaniel's mantra is 'You CAN improve your writing.' If you want or need to become a better writer, you need this book. *Words at Work* will help you banish your fears of writing while providing you with all the tools you'll need to confidently tackle any writing task you're called on to handle."

—Peter Bowerman, Author
The Well-Fed Writer series, www.wellfedwriter.com

"*Words at Work* is fabulous, fabulous, fabulous. I couldn't put it down. I'm going to recommend it in my writing and graduate-reading courses. It's so readable, and the style is lively and thoughtful. *Words at Work* is a perfect example of what Lynda is talking about—and she obviously knows what she's talking about. I just love it."

—Dr. Irene Willis, educator, author, and poet;
most recent collection, *Those Flames.*

"For those of you out there ready to take the leap, and ratchet your writing capabilities up to the next level, I've got just the book for you! *Words at Work* contains twelve chapters of great advice on how to become a better writer. I love her mantra that 'good writing is really good editing' and that even the best writers fight their way through multiple drafts before a final polished product emerges."

—Matt Youngquist, expert in the field of career coaching and
professional employment. Founder of Career Horizons,
www.career-horizons.com Bellevue, Wash.

*continued...*

"As a professional, I have had the opportunity to read and use the wisdom from many self help books and the key is finding one that is timely, doesn't demean and is immediately useful. McDaniel achieves this... [She] shows you how to see your writing through the eyes of others, how to target your audience and how to make more out of less... Whether you are just starting out, well seasoned or just wondering if your style is helping or hurting, *Words at Work* will give you the answer."
—Gregory J. Saunders, Allbooks reviewer

"What's wonderful about *Words at Work* is how grounded in real-life experience it is. No hocus-pocus or hokum. It's a valuable resource for those who want to improve their business and professional writing. And it was a nice refresher for me too! (I'm a professional writer/editor)"
—Anne Simpkinson, online managing editor
www.Guideposts.com

"Creative writing takes time and talent; but the basics can be learned. *Words at Work* will equip executives and creative types alike with the tools to make their writing come alive."
—Andrew Glasgow, Executive Director
American Crafts Council, New York, N.Y.

"*Words at Work* is an awesome book that will become my writing bible."
—Robin Andrews, communications expert
Foster City, California

# WORDS
## AT
# WORK

**Powerful business writing delivers increased sales, improved results, and even a promotion or two. A veteran writing coach shows you how.**

## Lynda McDaniel

ASSOCIATION FOR CREATIVE BUSINESS WRITING

Published by the
ASSOCIATION FOR CREATIVE BUSINESS WRITING
109 Sierra Drive
Walnut Creek, CA 94596

First edition: July 2009

Library of Congress Control Number: 2009905859

McDaniel, Lynda
     Words at Work : powerful business writing delivers
     increased sales, improved results, and even a promotion
     or two : a veteran writing coach shows you how /
     Lynda McDaniel. -- 1st ed.
       p. cm.
     Includes bibliographical references and index.
     LCCN 2009905859
     ISBN-13: 978-0-615-304267
     ISBN-10: 0-615-304265

     1. Business writing.  2. Success in business.  I. Title.
     HF5718.3.M33 2009       808'.06665

*To all the editors who helped me along the way.*

# Contents

# Contents

# Words at Work

# Introduction

Does writing well still matter in a time of e-mail, text messages, and Twitter?

You bet it does.

Writing is so much more than stringing words together. The process of writing can help you clarify your thoughts and uncover ideas you didn't know you had. Writing well can deliver increased sales, improved results, and even a promotion or two.

I admit that as a professional writer for 25 years and a business writing coach for five, I'm hopelessly in love with words: their flow, their nuance, their message. At the same time, I appreciate what a boon to business e-mail and text-messaging can be. Quick questions, fast answers, no postage—I'm all for them! But somewhere along the way, we're losing our ability to write. And something deeper...something more vital.

I couldn't put my finger on how to express just what we're missing when we can't write well so I did a brainstorming exercise I teach my students and clients called Brain Dump (See Chapter Two). I wrote for 10 minutes without stopping, and after some obvious ramblings, I came up with: "How is bad writing different from walking around unkempt? How is sloppy language different from not washing your hair or bathing? Or being rude in public?"

I liked that. In our e-world, we write to people who've never met us and maybe never will. To them, our typos and clunky phrases are like greasy hair and spinach between our incisors. They get the wrong impression of us, right?

I kept writing: "If people only knew how much writing helps them. It's not just some annoying task, it's the key to getting what they want." Now, I was getting warmer. When you write more than a quick e-mail or a brief text message, you start to build a relationship with your readers. You connect in a way that text-messaging, unless you're already the best of friends, can never deliver. Later, when issues arise or misunderstandings threaten, that stronger relationship will help you work through them.

Finally, just before the timer went off, I wrote: "Don't we lose access to our creativity when we write in spurts and sputters? Writing is the portal to our thoughts, and how can we get there in 140 characters?" That was it! What really troubles me about all this slap-dash writing is that it cuts off the creative process. Every invention, every good idea was first pondered and perfected through writing. When you write only short e-mail and text messages, your ability to develop your thoughts shrivels, along with your ability to persuade, sell, teach, improve, guide, change, contribute, and create.

*Words at Work* is about learning how to tap into your deepest thoughts and present them in an organized and compelling way. It's about thinking big and writing big.

## The big picture

I recently visited a Web site promoting leadership training. Curious about what skills were taught, I typed "writing" in the search box. The search engine sputtered for a moment and posted: "Did you mean 'working'?" No, I meant writing. I tried again with "writing skills." This time I got: "no results." And without writing skills, that's exactly what you get: no results.

When I started writing, I wish someone had shared these ideas with me:

1. Everyone can learn to write well.
2. Bad writers just stopped too soon.

I know both to be true. I see how they played out in my career, and as a business writing coach, I see how they hold true for my clients. Especially once they get the big picture.

What's the big picture? Not all the I-dotting and T-crossing we tend to think of as good writing. Oh sure, that's important, but there are plenty of books to help with that. What really matters is the ability to develop your ideas in an organized and creative format that respects what your readers need to know. If your best ideas come with a misplaced modifier or a few punctuation errors, so what? We can easily fix that. What's harder to do is develop something fresh—a solution to a problem, a marketing idea, a new approach—and write it with an exciting beginning, a fact-filled middle, and a compelling ending.

Now, don't get me wrong. Syntax and punctuation are important. That's why I've written a companion work-book, *Words at Work-book*, which covers grammar and punctuation in more detail. But *Words at Work* is about more than that. It's about creative business writing.

**"They sure don't teach this in school!"**
*Words at Work* shares every trick of the trade I know. I learned them as I carved out a writing career that included

just about every kind of business document—press releases, sales letters, reports, proposals, annual reports, catalogue copy, Web content, scripts, newsletters, blogs, e-mails, and magazine articles.

I get a kick out of hearing my students exclaim, "They sure don't teach this in school!" Many topics we cover in class—and now in *Words at Work*—are different from those in most business writing courses or books. They include:

- @ Eureka!—how to find your creativity and improve your writing.
- @ Stories—why they work and how to write them.
- @ Projection—what it says about you and your writing.
- @ Deconstruction—how to learn by studying other writers.
- @ Bad writers just stopped too soon—how to edit quickly and effectively.

Each chapter starts with a short story from my life that illustrates a key issue about the writing process: listen to your gut, write for your reader, overcome your fears of starting, tap into your creativity, edit your way to success, to name a few. More often than not, I learned these lessons by overcoming obstacles in my path. Over the years, I've come to appreciate the benefits of my bumpy road. My clients tell me that my stories inspire them, that they feel they can learn to be good writers too. And they do.

I've had plenty of overcoming to do thanks to the disapproving childhood too many of us experienced. You know, the kind with frustrated parents, prissy teachers, condemning preachers—the list goes on. But eventually we grow up, early or later, it doesn't matter. At some point, we're able to acknowledge our own inner critics—the ones we're keeping alive—and finally put them in their place. And sometimes we can even put them to work for us.

## Why this book is needed now

I grew up hearing the phrase "American ingenuity." It meant the world to me. It meant my country was a beacon of hope to the world, offering innovations and solutions to pressing problems. I don't hear it much anymore. Sure, there are still pockets of creativity, but we've lost our edge in so many arenas.

Writing can help get that back. As the portal to your thoughts, writing opens the way for you to ponder, study, delve, improve, innovate, and succeed. Trouble is, many people are so consumed by fears of writing, they can't even get started. As a business writing coach, I often see grown people quake at the thought of having to write something. They fear the censure of a boss, the derision of their peers, or the painful reminder that they lack some of these basic skills. Based on techniques I use in my practice, *Words at Work* can help them—and you—succeed.

## No excuses

"But I wasn't an English major," my clients plead. Well, neither was I. Frankly, I had no idea I wanted to be a writer. I didn't write for my high school newspaper or pay that much attention in English class. The only clue I had that I enjoyed writing was the way I finished my term papers early, something that usually got me a good grade (and no dates to the prom). It took 10 more years before I started my writing career. And more years than that to get the words right.

"I have a fear of writing," some reluctantly admit. Of course you do. We all do. Empty screens and blank sheets of paper are a writer's nightmare. I'll show you how to get rid of those demons, or at the very least use them to your advantage.

"I don't have time," others say. Not necessarily. Most of us were not taught how to write *efficiently*. I'll show you how to better use the time you have.

I wanted to share what I've learned the hard way so that maybe it would be a little easier for you. But, of course, writing isn't easy. Not for most of us. So don't get discouraged when you run into a rough patch. Or when your first draft stinks. Just keep writing. Like I said, bad writers just stopped too soon.

**Inspiration and motivation**

Maybe the best feature in *Words at Work* is the hope and encouragement I liberally provide. For starters, I want you to know that writing is not something you had to be "good" at in school or that you had to study for four years in college (though I'm not discouraging that). I urge you to leave your self-doubt behind and just get started. Writing well is more a matter of mindset than talent or gift. As you write, you gain confidence and discover new ideas and insights—and there's no telling where that can lead.

All stories in *Words at Work* are true. Some names have been changed to respect people's privacy.

# How to use this book

You've got what it takes. You wouldn't have this book in your hands if you didn't want to learn more. When you apply the tools and techniques presented here, you will know how to organize information creatively (no tedious outlines!); cut the fat (editing tips and tricks); and write in a clear, conversational style that makes people *want* to read your writing.

## Step by step

Whether you're a CEO or VP of Sales, administrative assistant or customer-service rep—*Words at Work* is designed to help you get the words right in everything you write. Like those holiday cookie recipes that, with a little tweaking of ingredients, yield six or seven different types of cookies, the techniques in *Words at Work* help you write dynamic:

- Letters
- E-mail
- Blogs
- Articles
- Reports
- Brochures
- Newsletters

- Sales materials
- Training materials
- Web content
- Direct mail
- Press releases
- Résumés
- Cover letters, and much more

While formats vary, the principles of well-written letters or blogs, for example, are the same as those for well-written reports or articles. You won't get confused over one technique for letters, another for reports, and so on. Like my students and clients, you'll feel confident you have the tools to write any and all business documents.

*Words at Work* is packed with benefits. As you work through it, you'll learn how to:

@ Overcome fear of writing. Break through writer's block so you can jump-start your writing—and your results. Fear confuses us. It makes us procrastinate—the biggest time-bandit of all. It makes us give up—if we're so bad at writing, why bother trying to be better? But when fear is banished, when we understand how powerful good writing can be, incredible things happen.

@ Communicate and connect with a wider audience to build your business or career.

@ Achieve goals faster through well-written letters and e-mail, reports and proposals, newsletters and blogs.

@ Build confidence. Right away, you'll realize you're already doing a lot of things right. Pretty soon, the tips and tools give you a new attitude about your writing.

@ Create new ideas. The writing process helps you tap into great ideas just waiting to be harvested.

@ Add extras for excitement. Learn techniques that set your writing apart.

@ Earn a promotion. Take time to write better, and someone at the top will notice. Text messaging? That's just top-of-the-head stuff. Ditto most e-mails. Good writing goes deeper. And who knows? Maybe someone will post it on the Web, and you'll get your 15 minutes (or more) of fame.

**Ground rules**

The rules are simple. To get the most out of *Words at Work*, here's all you need to do:

1. Keep writing. You'll create a powerful momentum.

2. Trust yourself. Please don't tell yourself how bad your writing is. We all start out with weak writing—we make it better through rewriting. Which leads to…

3. Understand that good writing is really good editing. This is so liberating. When I learned

that some of the best writers edit their work as many as 15 or 20 times, I knew I could do it too. Don't beat yourself up if your words aren't brilliant from the start. It takes time.

4.  Persevere. When you hit a snag, be kind to yourself. (In spite of my plea to the contrary, you're going to berate yourself. Whatever, keep writing.) Persevere with the process and keep using the tips and tools in *Words at Work* to create engaging letters, e-mail, reports, proposals, articles, Web content, blogs—whatever you need to write.

5.  Ignore the ornery editor rumbling around in your head. Mine still sits on my left shoulder and says the most unkind things, but I've learned to ignore him (till the time is right). Get used to telling him/her to take a hike (for now).

6.  Think of this book as training wheels—pretty soon you'll be rolling along on your own.

Now let's get started…

# Chapter One | Non Carborundum Illegitimus

My writing career started at the end of a gravel driveway lined with tall trees and sun-dappled daffodils. Although it was more than 25 years ago, I recall that day with the fiercest clarity: walking up to a massive oak door with a hand-forged handle, tugging on its surprising weight, and entering a world of art and craft, music and writing.

It was the most unlikely of places—just a speck on a map of the North Carolina mountains—but it was ripe with opportunity for me. With a pioneer's passion, I'd moved from Atlanta to a far-flung community called

Beaverdam. I was an eager participant in the back-to-the-land movement of the 1970s, naïve about what was in store for me yet bold enough to face it head on.

Eventually, property disputes forced me to move from Beaverdam to a wide spot in the road called Hanging Dog. The old farmhouse was so cold the butter was softer right out of the fridge than from the dish on the breakfast table. But that cold drove me out of the house into my warm truck to explore the region. I kept seeing signs for something called a folk school, and I finally followed the arrows to the John Campbell Folk School. That's where I met the director who eventually asked if I'd like to learn public relations. To be honest, I should have answered, "What's that?" Instead, I said, "Sure," and took to it like ink to newsprint.

I wrote all kinds of things for the school: newsletters and press releases, articles and ads. Once I saw my first published article, I was hooked. (An overworked newspaper editor printed my press release verbatim. I was too green to know that wasn't very good journalism.)

But after several years in the North Carolina mountains, I grew weary from the rigors of homesteading and holding down a full-time job. I was ready for a change from long days filled with chopping wood, harvesting beans, and putting food by. I loved each of those tasks, but collectively they left little time for the things I wanted to write.

I returned to Atlanta, where I quickly found that my writing experience carried as much clout as my sixth-grade penmanship award. The closest I got to writing was a clerical job at an ad agency owned by one of the maddest of the Mad Men. Ben had the persona of a cultured man but a heart of coal (at the very least, the black stuff ran through his veins).

It was a mean old place, like so many agencies. Egos clashed. Tempers flared. The top of the pecking order ruled, and I was at the bottom. I felt like a servant at a banquet, surrounded by a feast of color, words, and ideas that I couldn't sample. But I was determined to keep writing, so I garnered the courage to ask Ben if I could submit some copy—written on my time and my dime.

He looked startled. Then amused. "You?" he asked, walking away, shaking his head.

I left not long after that, bruised and angry. For months, I fostered fantasies of accepting a trophy at the Addy Awards while Ben sat in the audience, stunned. Silly of me, really. I should have thanked him for galvanizing my spirit. I haven't stopped writing since.

## Nothing to Fear But...

While living on my farm, I discovered a lot of things about writing by observing nature. My favorite lesson—there is a season for everything—taught me that there is a time to plan, a time to work, a time to rest, and a time to reap the rewards of all that effort. It makes perfect sense. No one sits down and writes something brilliant. It takes time pondering and planning, writing and editing.

I learned that writing is more like picking blackberries than huckleberries. Huckleberries, heavy bunches hanging low in August, fall into your bucket with the slightest nudging. Every now and then that happens with writing—the words just tumble out. But more often, writing is like picking blackberries—thorny patches keeping your ideas just out of reach. But keep stretching, and you'll get to the good stuff. Like that cobbler cooling on the windowsill.

Most of these obstacles boil down to fear. Fear of getting it "wrong." Fear of not finishing. Fear of finishing. And there's nothing unusual about that. Everyone feels—some more often than others—that fear of a blank screen or empty pad of paper.

Fear makes us think we have no interest in writing. Clients tell me they hate to write, but later I find that they're afraid to write because someone—their boss, client, or even that ornery editor in their own head—is standing by to criticize. It makes us freeze, procrastinate, even clean our offices before we write. But when that fear is lifted, when people understand how important writing is to their careers and that everyone can learn to write, incredible things happen.

Understanding your fear of writing is one of the fastest ways to overcome it. (Once people realize they're not alone, I see them change in as little as one hour.) Become aware of the critics inside and out. Stop worrying and fretting that people might pick your writing apart. Sure, some may do that. Those same people can also find fault with a warm, sunny day in December. Ignore them. *Non carborundum illegitimus.* Don't let the bastards wear you down.

### @ Plan more, write less

When Albert Einstein was asked how he'd go about solving a crisis if he had only one hour, he answered that he'd spend 55 minutes planning and 5 minutes executing. Professional writers agree. We know that we need to spend about 50 percent of our time planning, 20 percent writing and 30 percent editing. I'm not sure who held the stopwatch while we mulled over our projects, but those figures look right to me.

And planning helps you begin—which is the best way to overcome procrastination. Once you've got something on that blank paper or screen, you're on your way.

To get started, ask yourself:

1. Why is it needed?
2. How much detail do I need?
3. Who are my readers? Will they be reluctant? Resistant? Attentive? Passive?
4. What level of understanding will they bring to my document?
5. What do I want to teach them?
6. Are they my superiors? Peers? Employees?
7. What is their education level?
8. How long can I reasonably expect to hold their attention?
9. What length do I need? (Long enough to accomplish your goals but short enough to hold interest.)
10. Have I done all my research? Ask around. Get advice. Be a reporter—you don't have to be a genius and come up with everything on your own.
11. What's my deadline?

These questions will help you know what to include. If you're really stumped—or you've got too many ideas racing through your head—we'll soon explore Brain Dump, a great tool for getting your thoughts down on paper. All those ideas swimming in your head can contribute to procrastination. You think, "I'll start as soon as I'm clear on this." Good luck! You can't wait for clarity to strike—just get it down and then work to make your writing clear and concise.

## @ Get organized

### 1. The rule of one

First, a cardinal rule of writing: Effective writing has one idea per sentence, one idea per paragraph, one main topic per memo, letter, or e-mail. If you find you have more than one main topic—write another memo, letter, or e-mail. You want to keep your readers engaged, not confused.

### 2. The right approach

Next, choose an organizational method that gets the job done right. You can structure your business documents—whether they're letters and reports, newsletters or proposals—in a number of ways. Sometimes chronological order works; other times, you may want to use a point-by-point format. You can start in the present and use flashbacks to fill in important detail. (Here's the deal today, it actually started 10 years ago…)

- **Most important first:** This approach, which is the most common way to organize material, works well when writing letters, memos, reports, and proposals. Because you lead with your most salient information, you get to the point quickly and your readers know where you're headed. As a result, they're more likely to stay with you and remember your message.

- **Less important first:** If you only remember one point from this book, I hope that's "write to your reader." Don't just dump your information onto them. This organizing approach is a good example of respecting your reader—and, as a result, getting the results you want. Imagine how disastrous it would be if you started a memo telling your boss in the first sentence you need a raise. Or a new assistant. You've got to warm up your reader and build your case so that your request is a logical conclusion.

- **Chronology:** This step-by-step approach can be pretty dry. It's best reserved for meeting minutes, scientific reports, procedure manuals, etc.

- **Bad News Burrito:** Anytime you need to give less-than-pleasant news or criticism, try the Bad News Burrito. Write something positive, deliver the news, then roll it up with something positive. It's really just Psychology 101—and it can help you get the results you want. (This works especially well with employee evaluations.)

- **Compare & Contrast:** This approach works nicely for planning reports, feasibility studies, sales reports and letters, marketing reports—anything where you are making a case. State one side, then the other (e.g., advantages first, then disadvantages). Don't volley back and forth as you write. It feels like a tennis match—that you lose because your readers are confused, annoyed, or both.

- **Broad to focused or vice versa:** Knowing your audience's level of understanding will help you determine which to use. For example, consider an article on grammar rules. If I begin citing specific rules (focused) without explaining how these rules can help a general audience accomplish their goals (broad), they'll fall asleep on me. On the other hand, if I'm addressing English majors, they can appreciate the specific rules from the start.

Whatever approach you try, write from your heart—and to your readers. Talk to them like friends. As your sales jump and your reputation builds, you'll see your writing fears gradually slip away and a strong personal style emerge.

# Chapter Two | Eureka!

At first it was exciting to have stars walk through my office. Yul Brenner (elfin...who knew?). Rudolph Nureyev (naughty and nice). Itzhak Perlman (fiery yet compassionate).

After the ad agency, I got lucky and landed the public relations position at one of Atlanta's performing arts centers. Trouble was, my desk sat in the middle of the public entrance to the theatre. Everyone came and went this way—staff, board members, vagrants, delivery people, stars. Not to mention telephones ringing, board members pacing, and the boss's sycophant glaring (more on that in a minute). It was impossible to write with all that commotion. For a while, I took my writing home—I've never acquired the newsroom mentality—until I finally got a private office. I worked hard and did all right for myself, writing press releases, newsletters, playbills, and ads.

A year later, though, I was in a slump. Everyone worked hard there, and I hadn't found anyone with the time or inclination to brainstorm with me. My creative well was getting low. One particularly hectic morning—I was typing a press release and talking on two phones at once—I looked up at a stranger standing in the doorway to my office. His crooked smile mixed with admiration and amusement.

"You're pretty good at juggling," he said.

"Not by choice," I answered, wondering just who this guy was.

"I'm Jerry," he said, reading my thoughts. "I'm new here."

"Good to meet you, Jerry. I'm Lynda. I'm old here."

I soon discovered that Jerry was the most creative employee at the center. He had a quick wit and an excitement about the place no one could top. Maybe the theatre dazzled him more than most because he'd been somewhere darker than most. Jerry was an ex-con. And he'd just been hired as our janitor.

Jerry would stop by on his lunch break to help me with promotional projects. We'd brainstorm between bites of sandwiches from the next-door deli, and we turned out some great promotional copy over several months. Until my boss's assistant walked by my office and glared at us. Jerry and I just looked at each other. Somehow we knew that a great thing was about to end. Sure enough, the next day my boss told me if I was so creatively challenged I needed to consult with the janitor, maybe we'd better hire an ad agency. Which he did. Jerry went back to mopping. I stuck to PR. For a while. Eventually we both moved on to more creative environments.

That story still makes me sad, but you don't have to let something like that happen to you. I was young and unsure of myself. I should have stood up for Jerry—and myself—and reminded my boss of the good work we'd produced. I should have made sure that our creativity was encouraged and honored.

@          @          @

## UNLEASH YOUR CREATIVITY

Wherever you work, adopt an ironclad rule that everyone's contribution matters. Everyone's. Your company will be stronger when everyone feels a part of it. Listen to all perspectives. You'll tap into fantastic ideas that outshine surveys and focus groups any day.

And do Brain Dump. I wish I'd known about this technique back then. It gives you access to all kinds of ideas lurking in that marvelous brain of yours. Brain Dump is the perfect antidote to fear, dread, ennui, you name it. It gets you fired up to write, helps straighten out the tangle of ideas in your head, and taps into your creativity.

## @ Brain Dump 101

That word—creativity—causes a lot of people a lot of problems. The mere mention of it makes them freeze, something like panic flashing in their eyes. "Oh, I'm not creative," they say, quick to clear up that misunderstanding, just in case I thought they were capable of writing something more interesting.

But, I'm not talking about creativity like a giant jolt of electricity that lights up our lives once in a while (though that's great, too). I'm talking about a steady current that feeds us daily. The juice that inspires us to write a successful sales proposal, a persuasive proposal, or an interesting blog.

Brain Dump can get those juices flowing. Just set a timer and write without stopping for 10 to 15 minutes, depending on the length/depth of what you're writing. As your pen moves or your fingers tap the keyboard, don't stop! That's the key to the success of this technique. Keep writing no matter what. It's okay to fill in with "I don't know what to write" or "I'm writing about [*your subject*], I'm writing about [*your subject*]." Just keep writing—anything, though gently try to stay on track. When you do, something wonderful happens. That critical editor inside your head gets quieter with each tick of the timer. He steps aside and makes room for inspiration to strike.

### @ Science behind the art

I learned Brain Dump many years ago, and while I knew it worked, I didn't know why. An article by Jonah Lehrer in *The New Yorker* magazine cleared that up. Scientific research shows that our brains are busy coming up with innovative ideas while we go about our daily lives.

It works something like this: Our conscious brain is like a short-order cook at a diner: limited repertoire and limited capacity. No great insights start here, just your basic burger-and-fries ideas. But our prefrontal cortex, right behind our forehead, is like the executive chef of a fine restaurant—developing an inventive menu of ideas, organizing all the activity, and getting remarkable results. Our task is to help deliver this feast (our insights from the prefrontal cortex) to our conscious brain (which can really cook when inspired).

The most famous insight, the one that coined the expression we use today for this moment of discovery, is attributed to Archimedes, the Greek mathematician who was trying to work out the volume and density of the king's crown. When he got into his bath and watched the water overflow, legend has it, he shouted "Eureka!" (I have found it!).

The key to Archimedes' success was relaxation—he was stepping into a warm bath and not focusing on the problem. In addition to soaking in the tub or taking a shower, long walks in the woods and a good night's sleep also foster insights.

Personally, I find naps most enlightening, but unless you work in a home office, taking naps at work probably won't get you a promotion. At the office, you can take coffee breaks or go to lunch. You can let it rest overnight, if your deadline permits. And you can use Brain Dump right at your desk to get your brain to relax.

Softening our focus is critical. In *The New Yorker* article, John Kounios, a cognitive neuroscientist at Drexel University, explained why.

> *"You've got to know when to step back," Kounios said. "If you're in an environment that forces you to produce and produce, and you feel very stressed, then you're not going to have any insights. ... There's a good reason Google puts Ping-Pong tables in their headquarters*

*... If you want to encourage insights, then you've got to also encourage people to relax."*
-Lehrer, Jonah, "The Eureka Hunt," *The New Yorker,* July 28, 2008, page 44.

Brain Dump may seem as though you're focusing intensely on the subject, but it's different. It helps you relax, let down your guard, and tap into insights. Instead of forcing yourself to produce, you're opening your mind to vast possibilities.

To give you an idea what a Brain Dump looks like, here's an excerpt from one of mine—the one I mentioned earlier when I wanted an answer to the question about whether writing well, in the age of e-mail and Twitter, still matters. You'll notice I don't worry about spelling, punctuation, or syntax. I just wanted to capture new insights. And it worked (see underlined thoughts).

Okay, it's really important that we write better. The computer and e-mail have taken their toll on the Queen's English. I hate the way things have devolved. We say things curtly to each other with no softness, so consideration, no encouragement. Yes. No. OK. It's all so fast and free. Good writing doesn't have to take that much longer. It's more about caring. It's more about needing to do it right. It's about something deeper than just convention. I mean, isn't it like walking around unkempt? How is sloppy language different from not washing your hair, or bathing? Or being rude in public? Of course, a lot of that is going on too, but we just cannot devolve like that. Decorum. It matters. The right words matter. In the business setting it is important for both internal and external communications. How we speak to one another and how we speak to our clients and the outside world. If sloppy words come across someone's desk, that does not instill confidence in the person who sent it. It can make the difference between lawsuits and sales and whether or not someone is convinced. This means sales and bottom lines and prestige and status too. Good English can make all the difference.

Give it a try. Pick something you want to write (though Brain Dump is also a lifesaver for projects that have you stumped). Next, set a timer for 10 to 15 minutes. The timer is essential—if you have to stop to check your watch or worry about what time it is, the creative spell is broken.

One more thing: A lot of people do Brain Dump on their computers, their fingers flying across the keyboard to keep pace with the rush of ideas. Some prefer writing longhand on a legal pad. And others like to do Brain Dump on index cards or Post-it notes. They can move these cards/notes around and see how different approaches work. (This works particularly well for highly visual people.)

Each time you try this exercise (and I urge you to use it often, increasing the time as you grow more comfortable), take a minute before you start the timer to get clear on your purpose, your audience, and the strategy you want to pursue. If you don't know before you begin, that's okay too. Brain Dump will help you map out your direction.

## @ Find the nuggets

When you finish your Brain Dump, go back over what you wrote, circling the nuggets—the good stuff you got down. These are your key points. You'll find that Brain Dump helps you think, explore, and get beyond the obvious. I've yet to do a Brain Dump that didn't result in something exciting. Sometimes small. Often big. Always interesting.

Circling the nuggets looks like this:

Okay, it's really important that we write better. The computer and e-mail have taken their toll on the Queen's English. I hate the way things have devolved. We say things curtly to each other with no softness, so consideration, no encouragement. Yes. No. OK. It's all so fast and free. Good writing doesn't have to take that much longer. It's more about caring. It's more about needing to do it right. It's about something deeper than just convention. I mean, isn't it like walking around unkempt? How is sloppy language different from not washing your hair, or bathing? Or being rude in public? Of course, a lot of that is going on too, but we just cannot devolve like that. Decorum. It matters. The right words matter. In the business setting it is important for both internal and external

As you sort through the words, you'll find plenty of chaff you need to sift out. Don't worry. It wasn't a waste. Even the rejects are part of the creative process that led you from one point to the next. Circle your favorite words in your Brain Dump, such as that idea about how your motorcycle is like a dolphin. Or those breakthrough thoughts about the way your product saves time and money. Or just a word: ebullience. Where did that come from? Who cares—it's the perfect word for your report. Don't worry about how you're going to use the nuggets, just circle them. As for the stuff you don't circle for this project, some of it is just chaff. But some of it may be worth saving for inspiration later on.

### @  Create an Organic Outline

When you're done circling, assign each nugget a number. No. 1 should be the best information for the lead, or the beginning of your document. Find something that will grab your readers' attention. No. 2 represents the start of the nut graph (reporter's jargon for the meat of the document), No. 3 the next important, and so on.

Based on my Brain Dump and Nuggets, my Organic Outline looks like this:

1. Sloppy language
2. Computers & e-mail
3. The right words matter
4. Instill confidence
5. Get promotions – not lawsuits
6. Won't take much longer

I like this organic form of outlining because it evolves from the material. You can still use Roman numerals and all those letters and indentations if that suits your personality. For me, traditional outlines are just another form of procrastination.

When you're done, you'll have a working outline to help you organize your document. All in less than 20 minutes! And if you find that you've left something out, you can always add to it. Or do another Brain Dump to fill in any blanks. There's no limit to how many times or how long you practice this technique. The only limits are the ones we impose on ourselves.

## Chapter Three | The last word on first drafts

**A**nyone who takes a more creative path is bound to encounter naysayers, usually people too afraid to do it themselves or too insecure to accept others. Try to ignore them. Forge ahead and study everything you can get your hands on. Learn from your mistakes, and keep going.

Of course, that's easy for me to say now. For years, I suffered in silence. I was embarrassed that I was self-taught, and the word "writer" just stuck in my throat. Who was I to call myself a writer? I was an imposter, and I had the proof: My first drafts were terrible. Abysmal, really.

Somehow I kept writing in spite of this self-talk, but it wasn't easy.

Especially since doubts about my writing attracted critics like flies to stink. Like the time I helped plan and promote a major exhibition, CHINA: 5,000 Years of Discovery, presented by Georgia Institute of Technology as part of its centennial celebration. I contributed a long article about our success (the show was a city-wide hit) to the campus newspaper. Putting my byline in front of all those PhDs intimidated me, so I sought some help before submitting the article to my editor. I asked an English professor I knew at a small college if I could hire her to critique my work. She looked over my article, handed it back, and said, "Too much passive voice." (I had to look "passive voice" up in the dictionary—and we'll explore it in a few pages.) That was all she'd say. Curious. Next, I asked one of my bosses to review the article. He handed it back and said, "Too laudatory." (I had to look that one up too!)

Now that I think about it, they were probably right. I had lapsed into too much of both. But remember what I said earlier about not getting bogged down with small issues? This article had a big focus that had a lot of good things going for it. It needed help, but not CPR.

These negative critiques might have caused me to give up on the story (and further delayed my writing career), but from somewhere inside I heard *"Non carborundum illegitimus.*" In the face of negative comments, ponder the critique and plow ahead anyway. So what if something you write isn't a candidate for a Pulitzer? Have you ever seen early Woody Allen movies? Or listened to Mozart's first sonata? (Okay, he was only seven years old, but still...) You have to cut your teeth where you currently are. And hang in there long enough to have a breakthrough, like I did in the mid-1990s.

That's when I read a new book: *Bird by Bird* by Anne Lamott. All those years of agonizing over my embarrassingly bad first drafts, and in an instant I was cured. What I learned from Anne is that just about everyone writes terrible first drafts! Who knew?

Anne gave me permission to let myself go. Now, I let the words come any way they want (a real boost to creativity) because I know I can fix them later. All you have to do is write and write. Just get your ideas down. You can always go back two, five, fifteen times and make it better with each edit. In fact, don't think of your first draft as writing—it falls more under the planning/organization phase than writing. Capture that jumble of thoughts so you can wrestle with it and turn it into something great.

The process of writing is a lot like making a good loaf of bread. At first, all the ingredients you pull together are lumpy (rough draft). With a little mixing and kneading, it becomes smooth and elastic (editing). Next, it's time to let it rest (take a break). Come back later and punch it down (edit again), and let it rest again. Just before baking, brush it with a little egg wash for a shiny crust (final polish).

Early on, I served loaves of bread that could have doubled as doorstops. With practice, I got better at it. Same with writing. Thinking you should be able to sit down and write something wonderful is like expecting a wet glob of flour, water, and yeast to bake into a delicious loaf of bread. It doesn't happen that way. It takes time. It takes patience. It takes work.

I still mentally thank Anne Lamott for sharing this insight. And today, I can help my students and clients relax enough to write their terrible first drafts, though it takes some soothing and coaxing. But when they get it, they thank me too.

@        @        @

## A CHORUS OF VOICES

In Chapter One, I mentioned a season for everything. That certainly applies to ornery editor (OE). Who's that? As if we don't get enough grief from bosses and know-it-alls, most of us carry around this voice inside our head, the one making annoying—even crippling—remarks like, *"This is really bad. You'll never get this article sold. Man, how can you keep doing this? You ought to quit!"* And, of course, he picks on your first drafts.

While I learned that I can't make my OE go away, I've trained myself to ignore him while I'm writing early drafts. That's essential. You need the space to experiment and try again. Keep your OE as far away from the writing process as possible. Otherwise he'll do his best to make you give up or churn out something tried and true like everyone else.

But I also learned that I needed to let my OE back in during my editing process. That's when he just might have something valuable to say. *"That's too long. That doesn't feel right. Something's clunky. I don't think your readers will understand that. Can't you find a more exciting verb than 'is'?"* I can't tell you how often, when I felt tired or lazy, I'd ignore his promptings—usually an uneasy feeling in my gut about a certain paragraph—only to have an editor criticize that very paragraph.

At first, it may feel impossible to plug your OE in at the right time, but keep trying. Cling for dear life to your creativity and self-esteem while he's complaining early in your writing process. Then invite him over when it's time to edit. (More in Chapter Ten.) Even then, keep an eye on him. He's not always right, but he can draw your attention to some areas for improvement. Listen carefully. He really can be quite charming sometimes.

### @ Passive Voice

Since I just brought up passive voice, let's take a look at it. It's one of those concepts you often hear bandied about but don't necessarily know what it means. Once you get a handle on this culprit, you can easily add life to your writing.

What is passive voice? The Headless Horseman of writing. Simply put, passive voice occurs when no one or nothing seems to be responsible for the action.

(Passive) The new Web procedures were established. (By whom?)

(Active) The IT manager established new Web procedures.

(Passive) Women executives were discriminated against.

(Active) The board of directors discriminated against the women executives.

**How to spot it**

To determine if you're using passive voice, try these 1-2-3 steps.

#1 Look for the who or what the sentence is describing.

#2 Then find the verb of the action.

#3 Is the subject of the verb even in the sentence?

If so, is it actually doing the action?

(Passive) A strong push forward was made. (What's doing the pushing?)

(Active) The sales team made a strong push forward. Or, The sales team pushed forward.

(Passive) The verdict was given. (Who gave the verdict?)

(Active) The jurors delivered their verdict.

In this last example, not only is the active version more interesting, the verb "delivered" is more vivid than "was."

**Clear and concise**

Clarity is another reason to avoid passive voice. In the last example, did the judge give the verdict? The jury? It's clearer when someone or something is responsible for the action.

Active voice is also more concise. It gets right to the point, rather than making the reader plow through convoluted phrasing.

(Passive) There are lots of ideas she made up.

(Active)  She developed many ideas.

(Passive) The girl was struck by the bus.

(Active)  The bus struck the girl. (Much stronger—
you can almost feel the impact!)

## Exceptions to the rule

Of course, every rule has exceptions. About 10 percent of the time, passive voice is useful, especially when you don't want to embarrass or blame someone. For example: "Mistakes were made." That works because you don't want to point out that Joe or Jane goofed. (Not surprisingly, this is also referred to in Washington political circles as "the past exonerative" so no one has to take responsibility!)

Or consider this example: "The green light was given." That's okay if we don't need to know who gave the go ahead. (Sometimes we can get bogged down with unimportant information.) But if we need the clarity and/or accountability, we could rewrite that sentence: "The HR manager gave the green light."

And here's the most common exception: Technical and academic writing is filled with passive voice. It's expected. Check with office protocol before you begin a personal campaign against passive voice. I had to come to terms with this. As a result, I no longer accept coaching jobs with writers of technical reports or academic papers.

# Chapter Four | Looking inside out

**H**oward Pousner is one of the best journalists I know. I got to know him during my PR stint at the performing arts center, and we became friends. I always looked forward to meeting him in the lobby of the *Atlanta Journal-Constitution* before heading out to lunch. He usually ran late (deadlines and last-minute changes are a way of life for journalists), which was fine by me. That gave me time to study the lobby walls covered with old photographs capturing the long gone days of linotype and 20-column-inch articles. It felt like a hallowed hall to me—and it is. The Fourth Estate is as important to democracy as voting.

Journalism is a grand profession, even if today it suffers from too much corporate ownership, too many bean counters, and too few subscribers.

I loved it when Howard called to read me his latest article before it was published. He was no fool; he knew I was a great audience. I savored his engaging leads (beginning paragraphs) and all the clever wordplay he created without losing the integrity of his story. I also enjoyed tagging along to get-togethers with his newsroom mates.

I thought they were smarter and funnier than everyone else. And, generally they were, but there was something deeper going on here. I was projecting onto them. They were all fine journalists, but I now know that I also imbued them with a love of words that was *inside me.* My fascination with them was a message from my executive chef. She was trying to connect me with my own longings.

Projection, according to the Swiss psychiatrist Carl Jung, is an automatic process in which the contents of our own unconscious are perceived to be in others. Another way of putting that: It's as though we have a slide show inside our brains that we don't know exists. Every now and then, a worthy screen shows up (like my journalist friends) that turns the projector on. The screen lets us watch our inner slide show, and if we're paying attention, we can learn a lot about ourselves from what we're projecting. In my case, that was my love of writing, especially journalism.

Another classic example of projection is when we fall in love. We project our best traits and aspirations onto our loved ones. Just because we're projecting onto them doesn't mean they don't have all those fine qualities (though it takes discernment to determine if they do!). It just means that we need to own some of that gold too. Like my love of words.

Today, the term projection is more common, especially in talk shows and coffee-shop conversations. But it's usually used negatively. "She projected her shortcomings on me, and I couldn't take it any longer." "The President projected his need for approval onto the generals." But projection also can be a positive mirror of our inner desires.

To get to know yours, watch for your slide shows and become conscious of what holds special vitality for you. At work, pay attention to people you admire—and figure out why. Study books and reports you think are excellent—and think about why. Chances are you're projecting something important about yourself.

Once projection rears its head, it tends to rev up its message until we finally take notice. That's what happened when I left the arts center for the assignment with Georgia Institute of Technology's centennial celebration. This huge project included the blockbuster exhibition I mentioned earlier, CHINA: 5,000 Years of Discovery.

I worked with two other people—one, a left-brained bean counter, the other a right-brained creative—and I respected them both. Dick Sims, the creative one, was a veteran ad man, and unlike my first encounter with an agency guy, he became a beloved mentor. We wrote all kinds of materials together and interfaced with the PR agency that was handling the press releases and brochure for the Chinese exhibition.

I can still recall the feelings I had reviewing that brochure when it came over for our approval. It was sophisticated, clever, and engaging. Yet, all I could think about was how I could never have written it. Never mind that I had not yet devoted the hours to my writing skills that this copywriter had. Never mind that I hadn't fully explored what I *could* do as a writer. I just felt like an imposter.

More often than not, the slides are about our "becoming," i.e., something nascent inside of us that wants—and needs—to be developed. Because of the gap in desire and reality, the initial experience can be troubling. But these negative feelings can offer sage advice when we know what to do with them. Everything within us is part of the real deal, the whole person we're growing into. When I projected my self-doubt onto the creative brochure copy, if I'd known about projection, I could have understood how deeply important it was to me to write beautiful words. Instead, I held myself back by telling myself I was a loser.

If only I'd said, "Hey! It's time to study, practice, learn." What arrogance to think I should be able to sit down and craft thoughtful copy. What nonsense to believe it just flows out and doesn't require diligence and patience and plenty of editing.

That's one reason I've written this book. You don't have to make this mistake. Next time you have a strong reaction to something or someone, be happy even when the encounter feels uncomfortable. What change ever happens when we're completely at ease? Go inside and discover where that feeling is coming from. What do you really like or hate about it? What inside of you would like to be just like that or not at all like that? Either way you win.

@            @            @

## TOOLS OF THE TRADE

I learned a lot from those journalists and copywriters. I enjoyed picking up the paper and reading their articles. And once I realized how much journalism meant to me, I set about learning all I could from them. So, let's explore some of the best techniques journalism offers to writers in the business world.

**@ Inverted Pyramid**

EXCITING LEAD

NUTS & BOLTS

INFORMATIVE

OH REALLY?

NICE

OK

O

This journalist's tool looks like an upside-down pyramid—with the tip pointing down and the broad base at the top. It's a great icon to keep in mind as you organize anything you're writing—from a letter or e-mail to a report or newsletter article. It looks like what your document should look like—stacked right from the beginning with the best stuff on top and winding down to a well-rounded finish.

Referring to your organic outline, start at the top with your Nugget No. 1, for your lead, or beginning paragraphs. Next, Nugget No. 2 becomes the nut graph, or the nutshell paragraph packed with important facts, followed by No. 3. and so on. You want to make your points early to hook the reader. That way, if the readers' train arrived at the station or their boss stopped by for a chat, you've still made your point. (If you did your job right and grabbed their attention, they'll come back for more.)

This technique is particularly useful in publishing—your in-house newsletter, annual report, brochure, or news-paper/magazine article—because sometimes a story won't fit the space allotted. It's easier to lop off lower down where the information is less critical. And by the way, the O at the tip doesn't mean your closing is not important—but rather that you've developed the story full circle.

### @ Six Wise Men

The Six Wise Men are classic reporter questions: who, why, what, where, when, and how. With some exceptions, they all need to be answered to make your document complete. I use them as a safety net—if I've answered all six in my writing, I feel confident that I've covered all the bases.

## 1. Who

- Have you explained all the players? Who are you writing about?

- Know your reader so you can use the right tone. If you're writing for a board of directors or your boss, the tone is different from a report to a colleague. If you're writing for a news magazine, the tone may be different from a feature article.

- Make sure you've identified and explained who's who in your document.

## 2. Why

- The focus of your document. What are you writing about and why is it important? All readers ask, "What's in it for me?" Have you satisfied them?

- Once you've done Brain Dump, organize what you wrote based on your focus. Are you trying to convince someone of something? Are you apologizing for a mistake? Are you promoting the company softball team? (Even that needs good writing to convince people to sign up.)

- The purpose of your document—have you explained what it's all about?

## 3. What

- Know your subject and cover all the facts. Try to summarize the purpose of your document in your lead.

- When you go back to Brain Dump, ask yourself if you forgot anything. Often during the break from the writing, something will pop into your head.

- Being a reporter means you don't have to be a genius and know everything, which lifts another burden from the writing process. You can ask others for advice and insight. You can observe, interview, and research your subject in order to make it stronger and more interesting—both for you and your readers.

## 4. Where

- Know your format and length. Where will this be published? On the Web? (Web pundits used to say keep everything short for the Web, but that's changing.) For a newsletter? What space limitations do you face? You sure don't want to write and edit a great article, only to have it cut in half (though that can happen even after the best preparation).

- If appropriate, where is the action taking place? What are the logistical details?

## 5. When

- Know your deadlines and stick to them. You'll earn the respect of editors and bosses, which will lead to better assignments and performance reviews in the future.

- If appropriate, when is the action taking place? What's the timeframe?

## 6. How

- What did it take to accomplish something? What monies, time, and effort were involved?
- What kind of call-to-action do you need to get the results you want?

Now that you've acquired some new tools, let's look at a way to improve your writing by copying others. (And I'm not talking about plagiarism.)

# Chapter Five | Tear it apart!

**M**y mentor, Dick Sims, had been at the top of his game for years. He'd won awards, dealt with bigwigs, and written reams of thoughtful copy. He was secure in his knowledge and creativity, so he didn't mind sharing.

Dick believed in me and showed me how to write better. He was the best business friend I've ever had— and he continues to be a model for my business coaching. Today, I try to help anyone who asks—and when I do, I always come out the winner. I learn as much from them as they do from me. Just as Dick helped me focus on what I could do (instead of what I thought I couldn't do), I helped Dick remember what it feels like to really care about your work again. Together, we did something bigger and better than anyone thought we could. (We attracted more than 425,000 people to CHINA: 5,000 Years of Discovery in just four months.)

And remember the exhibition brochure I loved/hated while working on that exhibition? That brochure was a gold mine of creativity tools, if only I'd known them at the time. In addition to what it taught me about projection, it was a perfect example for what I now call "deconstruction."

The inspiration for deconstruction struck while I was visiting an art museum. The text panel explained that Degas and Cassatt applied for permits to the Louvre to copy the Great Masters. I was stunned. It had never occurred to me that it was okay to copy greatness. Wasn't that cheating? Weren't we taught in school never to copy? For writers, doesn't that edge dangerously close to plagiarism?

Eventually, though, I realized that deconstruction, like artists at the Louvre, was simply an exercise, not a finished product. Degas and Cassatt developed their own unmistakable styles—they just wanted to practice techniques and prime their creativity at the same time. We learn by example, by mimicking greatness until it feels natural to us.

To translate that for writing, instead of envying other writers, I needed to take a closer look at what I admired about their work. I needed to study greatness. While teaching myself to write, I spent hours poring over books and magazines. I made copious notes of how the writers handled their information. I earmarked pages until the magazine didn't close right.

As for that exhibition brochure, if I'd understood deconstruction back then, I would have known to tear it apart and admire it under a magnifying glass. Savor every one of those delicious verbs the copywriter chose. Examine how he organized it. Study the tone and flow. What kind of structure did he use? How did he end it?

Now I've learned to rejoice when I read something of beauty. First, it deserves it. Second, it's talking to me, it's my slideshow projecting a new level of accomplishment that I want to achieve.

Next time you read something that makes you happy, jealous, sad, envious—the emotion doesn't matter, it's all informative—deconstruct it. Here's what to look for:

1. How does it start?
2. What's in the middle?
3. How does it end? Is there a great call-to-action?
4. What about headlines/deks, subheads, pull quotes, bullets?
5. Check out the different types of sentence structures used.
6. Make note of the vivid verbs and colorful similes.
7. Any alliteration? Metaphors?
8. How about stories? Especially stories.

*The New Yorker* was and is my best source for inspiration. As I read, I glean ideas that I can bring to my business writing as well as my journalism. Find your own inspiration and try something different from your usual sources. If you read the *Economist*, for example, read the *New York Times* business section. Or better yet, the *New York Times* arts section. Take a different path and bring what you discover to your business writing.

And again, don't worry about your rough first draft. Degas and Cassatt didn't just pick up paint brushes and make masterpieces. They, too, made rough drafts—sometimes many of them—before they squeezed the first drop from their paint tubes.

Now, let's go over how to structure your documents and incorporate the techniques you discover through deconstruction.

@          @          @

## SIX ESSENTIALS OF STRUCTURE

When you've finished your planning and research, the following six elements of structure offer fresh approaches to business writing. They help you organize your documents and create a strong beginning, middle, and end.

### 1. Inverted Pyramid

We've already covered this tool. Keep this easy-to-remember icon in mind to help you start with the most important information and end with everything tied together. By the way, there are a few exceptions to this rule. As I mentioned in Chapter One, meeting minutes and chronological reports present what happened when. And those times when the so-called least important information is presented first, as in the case of asking for a raise or hiring an assistant. That's the most important thing to you, but it would be a mistake to put that in the first sentence. You've got to build your case. And when you think about it, those explanatory facts *are* the most important points to your reader—the *why* you deserve a raise. The raise or assistant are the most important to *you*.

### 2. Leads: Start with a bang!

You've got 10 seconds to catch someone's attention, so grab them with interesting stories, facts, and news. Forget "This letter is to inform you…" or "This report will outline…" And don't ever start with something like, "In accordance with Statute # 54 of the City Code…" Governments love that one. No wonder people throw away letters like that, mumbling something unprintable about bureaucracies.

Below are a few examples of different types of leads. They may seem an unconventional start to a letter or report, proposal or Web content, but they grab attention. Whatever approach you take, remember to make your point quickly. You don't want to "bury your lead," a phrase borrowed from journalism that means your most important point didn't surface till deep within the sixth paragraph.

**Tell a story...**

*Edith Ball was only nine years old when she first dreamed of a clinic. It was a vivid dream, a response to more suffering than any little girl should see—babies dying from dysentery, young lives succumbing to tuberculosis, and her own mother almost bleeding to death as Ball stood by, helpless...*

**Make it up...**

*Step into the department-store elevator just ahead, where the uniformed attendant waits near the polished brass grille to give us a quick trip through the history of retail restaurants...*

**Compare/contrast to something familiar...**

*If Thomas Edison had to answer to a board of directors, would we still be reading by candlelight? Or would our homes and businesses have been illuminated a decade earlier if he had worked with an informed, supportive board? The help-or-hinder question continues to burn...*

## Ask a question...

*We learn what we don't know through research and study. But how do we learn what we don't know we don't know?*

## Observation...

*It's 8 a.m., and a work crew dressed in jeans and sport shirts just arrived at Casa Vasquez. Inside, they roll up their sleeves and scatter, some tackling the walk-in cooler, others arranging cleaning schedules. Perhaps this isn't the typical image of a restaurant consultant, but it's the way Gina Jones likes to work.*

## Looking back...

*Before Nintendo and all the after-school activities, even before Fisher-Price, kids just played. They turned on their imaginations as they turned over cardboard boxes and entered a world of forts and dollhouses and puppet shows. Emily Willis recalls those times...*

## 3. Solid middle

You've done your research, organized your thoughts, and started writing. Now pack your middle full of the Six Wise Men (who, what, where, when, why, and how). Put all your most important facts here. As a rule, keep paragraphs short—with only one idea per paragraph.

## 4. Headlines, deks, & subheads

*"On the average, five times as many people read
the headline as read the body copy."*
-David Ogilvy, *"Father of advertising"*

## Headlines

A well-written headline attracts attention and conveys a summary of what's ahead. These are typically found in magazine and newspaper articles, but a creative headline (usually highlighted in bold) can add excitement to any business document. Next, when space or format allow, add a dek, those often-italicized words that clarify the headline.

### Not Just On Time—Ahead of Time
*Pace Real Estate Group brings in projects
early and below budget.*

### Below the Beltway
*Memories of this century's fabulous scandals—
past and present—are as much a part of our
nation's capital as the Lincoln Memorial.*

## Subheads

Have you ever opened a page of copy so dense you felt tired just looking at it? Give your readers some breathing space with subheads, and they're more likely to keep reading. Subheads break up the page, add interest, and create a little white space, which is like fresh air for your readers.

Subheads also help impatient readers who cannot (won't?) take the time to enjoy an entire document. If you can't beat 'em, join 'em—give them something that grabs their attention as they skim. Subheads, too, should be in boldface.

## 5. Sidebars & sidekicks

### Sidebars

In today's "quick read" world, your sidebars—those boxes in magazines and newspaper that contain relevant lists, addresses, contact information, or key points usually set off by bullets or numerals—often get more attention than the body copy. As you work with your material, think about what information is better suited to a sidebar. One of my favorite examples covers customer service—a list of dos and don'ts entitled: *CARP at Your Customers* (which would catch any reader's eye). CARP is an acronym for four pointers: the first started with the letter C, the second A, and so on.

### Sidekicks: pull quotes, bullets, and numbers.

- Pull quotes—pithy quotes from the body of the story often set in large letters—add eye appeal and draw attention to an important comment. Look for copy that sums up the gist of your document. And pull quotes don't have to be actual quotes— you can use key points too.

From a story about the effects of Hurricane Katrina...
*"If you can imagine a 747 parked on your roof at full throttle for four hours, that was what Katrina sounded like."*

From a report about retaining good employees...
*"Money and power are not the prime motivators they once were. Job satisfaction, freedom, the*

*chance to make a difference—these are the new career drivers."*

@ Bullets, like those I'm using here, are a great way to set off copy and draw attention. They break up copy, make key points stand out, and cut out lengthy sentences no one will read anyway.

@ Numbers are even better than bullets because they also alert our brains to pay attention to a certain number of items. For example, when you have five points written in a narrative style, our brains tend to read only two or three points out of the five. In the case of e-mail, that means additional back-and-forth to get the job done. With other business documents, it may mean lost opportunities or, again, the need for more clarification.

## 6. Lasting impressions: End with impact

Close your document with a summary of key points and a bang-up ending so that readers remember your message. Try to get your ending to flow naturally from the facts and, ideally, refer back to your lead. Include clear instructions of what you want the reader to do: send money, reply by mail, e-mail or telephone, sign up, take part, contribute skills, and so on. Don't have a strong ending yet? Don't worry. You've still got lots of chances to get it right.

Work toward endings that:

- Leave a lasting impression.
- Make your expectations known.
- Give clear instructions for action.
- Finish any stories you've started.

Consider these examples of effective calls-to-action.

**Call today and save:** Make an offer with a deadline; add some benefits to seal the deal.

> *Register by December 21, 2009 and receive our e-workbook "Retain and Gain" absolutely free (a $59.99 value). Simply follow this <u>link</u> to complete our easy registration. Our train-and-retain programs can help you eliminate the headache and expense of losing good employees.*

**Pick and choose:** Offer a choice—and a recommendation. This e-mail presented four options and closes this way:

> *I recommend we select item #1. It's the best value and gives us more exposure at a great price. Please let me have your decision by March 30.*

**Ask for a commitment:** Deadlines and confirmations are essential.

> *We need your RSVP by November 30. Just call 206.555.5555 to confirm. We will send you additional information on how this program can improve your skills.*

**Finish your stories:** Here's how I ended the fundraising letter about Edith Ball:

*As for retirement, the mere mention of the word makes Ball wince. Besides, she can't stop now. Her dream isn't finished. She's planning a 24-hour emergency room with a 36-hour holding area. No ground has been broken, the first potluck has yet to be scheduled, but who can doubt that Edith Ball's latest dream is as certain to succeed as the one summoned by a little girl some 60 years ago.*

*Won't you help keep Edith's dream alive? Your contribution will ensure we can build the new wing at Walnut Grove Clinic and improve our services to all the residents. Please fill out the enclosed contribution card and return as soon as possible. Edith thanks you.*

One of the most important tenets of good writing is to use a clear, conversational style. Next, I'll share how I finally learned this lesson.

# Chapter Six|Corporatespeak

*"...plain talk will not be easily achieved in corporate America. Too much vanity is on the line. Executives and managers at every level are prisoners to the notion that a simple style reflects a simple mind. Actually, a simple style is the result of hard work and hard thinking...."*
-William Zinsser, On Writing Well, (page 154)

No way was I going back to a 9-to-5 job. After that big centennial project, I couldn't face the confines of a cubicle. That two-year contract had given me a taste of the uncertainties of self-employment—and the realization that I thrived not knowing exactly what was happening next.

A week after that contract ended, I launched Creative Pursuits, a writing and public relations agency. Of course, once I'd set up shop, I came face-to-face with all the realities of entrepreneurship, and that's where I got myself into a little trouble. Trying to fit in and appear as though I knew exactly what I was doing, I borrowed the style of the day, a bloated language now pegged as bureaucratese or corporatespeak.

At the time, consultants had to develop elaborate proposals before we got the job. Today, we call it unpaid consulting, and any salesperson worth her commission says, "No." But back then, it was expected, and as an inexperienced entrepreneur, I fell for it.

I read my competitor's proposals, and I tried to write like them. I jettisoned good writing and started making my proposals longer—and as the thinking went, better—with empty words like institutionalization, enhanced leverage, strategically secure, and deployment of managerial processes. (I cringe just typing that bombastic prose.) This was around the same time that I bought an oversized executive chair for my small home office. Some sort of fantasy was definitely playing out.

Fortunately, I couldn't keep it up. After a while, I was confident enough to shake off the last vestiges of that ridiculous writing and adopt a simple storytelling style. And I gave away that chair too.

## WRITE THE WAY YOU TALK

Today, as a business writing coach, I help people break off their love affair with six syllables when one works even better. I've read some paragraphs so convoluted I had to ask clients to explain what they were trying to say to their readers. When they start talking, their thoughts come out fresh and clear. I stop them before they forget what they just said and tell them, "Put that down!"

I keep a file of bad examples because some of them are unimaginable. You couldn't make it up if you tried.

> *1. "The purpose of this report is to clarify the communications endeavor we discussed and further develop the necessary components for review by the board, inasmuch as…"*

> *2. "The process, if accelerated through the strategic channels in the allotted timeframe, will leverage our deployment as an immeasurable uniqueness in the marketplace."*

Relax. Be yourself. Use plain English. Write in an open, honest style. Don't try too hard. Conversational writing is in. Large words and convoluted sentences don't get the message across. Just talk to your readers. In turn, you'll increase sales, eliminate misunderstandings, and achieve goals faster.

@ **Watch your tone**

- Match your tone to your audience. Just as you wouldn't use "parameters" and "moreover" when writing a friend, you wouldn't use "LOL" or "howdy" when writing a prospective client (unless you're the head of a rodeo talent agency).

- Tone can be tricky when you don't particularly like the reader. And it's awfully hard to find the most effective tone when you're annoyed with someone. In these situations, try writing to your best friend. Imagine her smile, her patience. Or the time she did that funny dance while listening to the radio. It works.

- And please give up outdated language and stuffy or wordy phrases. Keep it simple. Consider these before and afters:

  | | |
  |---|---|
  | *nevertheless* | but |
  | *utilize* | use |
  | *make use of* | use |
  | *with reference to* | about |
  | *subsequent to* | after |
  | *give consideration to* | consider |

- As much fun as it is to vent and fume as you write, it goes without saying that you need to delete any hint of inappropriate anger, sarcasm, or frustration. In fact, don't even write such things on your computer. The "delete" key does not destroy your rant—and in our litigious culture, you could put you or your company in jeopardy. (E-discovery is the 21$^{st}$ century equivalent of ambulance chasing.)

Consider this e-mail from a representative of a civic organization where I'd given several complimentary workshops. I'd written to ask if the CEO Roundtable, a group of business leaders who met monthly, ever needed speakers. An honest, straightforward question, right?

**Before**

> *Lynda:*
> *The CEO group makes the decisions on where they want to dig deeper. They have been adamant about not having disruptions and attempts to network and market from outsiders, which dilutes the value of their interactions. So, the speakers and guests have been very rare, and are approved by the group.*
>
> *I will note that you are available, and if the issue of executive coaching comes up, will call you. Thank you for your interest in the CEO roundtable.*

Looks like somebody got up on the wrong side of the bed. He may have been upset about something completely different, but he sure burned a bridge with me. Instead, the less-is-more approach works just fine.

**After**

> *Good morning, Lynda,*
>
> *Thank you for your interest in the CEO Round-table.*
>
> *The CEOs in the group decide where they want to dig deeper. While they sometimes invite guests, mostly they stick to the major issues they have come together to discuss.*
>
> *I will keep you in mind if the issue of improved business writing come up.*
>
> *Thanks again for your interest.*

Even if you have to grit your teeth, so what? At the very least, you won't be spotlighted as the "bad example" in a book someday.

### @ Negative nixes, positive persuades

Negative wording is an insidious problem. Since I've been teaching, I've realized how often I've used variations of the word "not." It's not intentionally negative, just a bad habit.

Negative wording stops us, while positive wording helps persuade. Consider these before and afters. The second column offers ways of saying the same thing in a more supportive way.

| | |
|---|---|
| *Don't do it that way.* | Try it this way. |
| *I don't like that idea.* | I prefer this idea. |
| *He did not remember.* | He forgot. |
| *I don't believe that.* | Is that right? |

Sandy Bjorgen, founder of Improv-able Results® in Seattle, taught me another way to turn a negative into a positive—and improve my results in both writing and speaking. Instead of saying "Yes, but…" try "Yes, and…" It sounds so simple, and it is! That's the beauty of it. The only hard part is weaning yourself from old negative language.

While coaching government workers, I saw how often they use negatives to tell people what they have to do. (And we all know how well that goes over!) Consider this example:

**Before**

*Councilman Smith asked me to respond to your recent letter seeking a donation of space for a plaque. I'm sorry that we cannot help.*

*The City's ability to make donations to non-profits is limited by our State Constitution, which prohibits local jurisdictions from giving away assets without offsetting compensation,*

*usually in the form of fair market value. Add-*
*itional rules and regulations restrict use of some*
*land for purposes other than that for which it was*
*acquired; for example, land owned by the City's*
*utility departments must be for utility purposes,*
*and the gifting of park land is prohibited by*
*local Initiative 42.*

**After**

*Councilman Smith asked me to respond to your*
*recent letter seeking a donation of space for a*
*plaque.*

*While the City's ability to make donations to*
*non-profits is limited by the State Constitution\*,*
*we have a few ideas that may help you find an*
*appropriate spot for the plaque. You might*
*want to consider:*

*1. Partnering with local service organizations*
   *such as Kiwanis or Rotary.*
*2. Talking to local garden clubs.*
*3. Placing the plaque in a City park or in a*
   *public right-of-way area without the City*
   *donating the space...*

And get those bulky and annoying statutes out of the
first paragraph and down at the bottom of page.

*Our State Constitution prohibits local jurisdictions from giving away assets without offsetting compensation, usually in the form of fair market value. Additional rules and regulations restrict use of some land for purposes other than that for which it was acquired; for example, land owned by the City's utility departments must be for utility purposes, and the gifting of park land is prohibited by local Initiative 42.*

You can't always say it positively (to wit: this sentence). But if you want people to do something differently—and not alienate them in the process—try to avoid "not" or "never" whenever you can. You're more likely to get the results you want.

# Chapter Seven | You first!

**D**ave Wilson was the silent type. He never seemed to work hard, but he was actually very busy—observing. The first time I met him at Alan David's photography studio, he didn't say a word, but I could tell he was paying attention. Later, he told me he was impressed that I had described an entire event I'd planned—a Viennese-style fundraiser from invitations to closing remarks—without any idea who my client might be. I think that's the only reason he later agreed to collaborate.

It's been ages since I've seen Dave, but I often recall what he taught me about observation and creativity. And that he wore a fedora when they were no longer cool. Or before they were cool again—I could never tell which kind of guy Dave was. But it didn't matter what he wore on his head, it was what was inside that fascinated me.

Together, we designed and wrote scripts for trade show booths. And we marveled at how people stood in long lines just to visit our clients' booths. Here's why: What really matters, Dave taught me, isn't what your product/writing does/says, but what it gives its audience. Solutions? Dignity? Strength? Time? Rest?

Two booths stand out in my memory. One, a truck-stop booth we created for a major trucking firm (where Dick Sims headed up marketing after the CHINA exhibit). Dave figured out how to solve an age-old problem at trade shows: Exhibitors want a lot of information from their visitors but visitors rarely want to spend the time to give it to them. So, we designed a booth where they would *want* to spend time. We drew them into the booth with coffee and doughnuts and friendly banter, and they stayed because of a humorous script Dave wrote packed with problem-solving information *they* wanted. (The booth won first place in that year's annual advertising contest of the American Trucking Association.)

Our longest lines crisscrossed the trade show floor to see the booth we designed for a home healthcare agency.

We had a lot of competition that year—slews of sales-people touting features like carnival barkers. Instead, Dave wrote a script for an actress who played Addie, an elderly woman who'd just returned home from the hospital. Add an easy chair, a table, a handful of "family" photos, and we were in business. Addie talked quietly about what it meant to be home, surrounded by the people and things she loved. I wove in company features that answered that all-important question every reader/viewer is asking: What's in it for me? Something all good business writing—from trade show scripts to blogs—needs to do.

@          @          @

# WIIFM - WHAT'S IN IT FOR ME?

That's what all readers are thinking, consciously or not. And you've got 10 seconds to convince them you understand their needs.

It's easy to talk about yourself, your products, and your services and assume that readers make the jump to how those features will benefit them. They don't. First, you need to ask, interview, and watch so you understand what they want and need. Then, you need to write *to* them, address *their* needs, concerns, and problems. As a result, you'll grab their attention and keep them engaged.

**How to get where you want to go**

Think of your writing as a bus making its way through traffic. All the best words and phrases are on board, along with your features and benefits. And the proper use of commas, periods, and dashes (like road signs) are making the ride smoother for your readers.

But who's driving the bus? If it's you (the writer), that bus is headed in the wrong direction. Put your reader in the driver's seat, and that bus is speeding toward the results you both need. As you let the reader drive your bus, you'll share benefits and results they care about (rather than all the features you're so proud of).

**Beginner mind**

In journalism, we learn to assume, "the reader knows nothing." I've heard others refer to this as the "curse of knowledge." Once you understand a concept or product, you can forget what it felt like before you'd acquired that knowledge. Without realizing it, you're writing way over your readers' heads—and you're going to lose them. Try to crank your mind back to beginner mind when you were introduced to the concepts you're writing about and write to your readers from that perspective. They'll understand your message much better. (This is also a great way to jettison jargon you've picked up along the way.)

**Grab attention from the get-go**

You probably don't realize how many people delete and throw away hard-to-read documents. I was shocked when scores of my students freely confessed they simply hit "delete" if something looks too boring or too dense. Shaping the lead to your readers' needs works wonders.

To keep your readers engaged, ask yourself:

@ What pains are your readers experiencing? Do you have answers for their problems?

@ Do you have a third-party story that *shows* how your product can help? (See Chapter Nine)

@ Are you offering something new or unique to your industry?

@ Can you make the readers' lives easier? Save them time or energy?

Study the following before-and-after example that turns a client's feature dump into a solution-oriented offer.

**Before**

> *Subject: We can help you improve customer service*
>
> *Dear Janice,*
>
> *Every business owner recognizes the import-ance of offering consistent, premium service by the highest-quality employees, and finding an objective method for evaluating employee service levels against client expectations isn't always easy to do. We help you discover if your employees are adhering to your company's service policies and delivering consistent levels of service. Jones Consultants offers a range of services designed to quickly and efficiently provide vital information on their performance. We can create a specially priced bundled pack-age of services, or you can selectively pick and choose just those services that fit your business needs.*

Whew! Lots of long sentences and jumbled thoughts from Jones's perspective. Let's try again from the reader's viewpoint:

**After**

> *Subject: Customer service you can be proud of*
>
> *Dear Janice,*
>
> *You consistently want to offer your customers the best service from courteous employees. But do you?*
>
> *At Jones Consultants, we work with clients who are worried about their employees' performance, tired of getting customer complaints, and frustrated with incomplete results. If that sounds familiar, we can help. We start by analyzing your business and customizing services to give you accurate information on your employees' performance.*

When you start any writing project, ask yourself what solutions you can offer your readers. Whether you're writing a letter or e-mail, report or proposal, keep WIIFM in mind to hold your readers attention.

# Chapter Eight | Wordplay

**M**y first published magazine article paid $50. Somehow I had the good sense to ignore the paycheck and pore myself into the assignment as though it were for *The New Yorker*. To research the story, I drove an hour to the town I was writing about and sat on a bench on Main Street and, like Dave Wilson taught me, just observed. I wasn't looking for anything in particular, just paying attention to details, like the woman watering the hanging baskets of petunias and the merchants sweeping their walkways. I ambled through a neighborhood and noticed that every home had a front porch. Here's what I wrote:

*Haywood County has a high percentage of porches per capita. While that statistic may never show up in a census report, it says a lot about the county and the people who live here. Wraparound porches on restored Victorian treasures, plain white porches fronting farm houses, long porches sweeping across downtown businesses—whatever the style, the message is the same as their rocking chairs creak in a slow, regular rhythm, "life is good here, life is good."*

*One California town recently legislated that porches must be included on all new homes, but in Haywood County, porches are already the law of the land. It's a legacy from days gone by that will serve residents well as this thriving county grows into its economic and recreational potential...*

That lowly clip garnered thousands of dollars when an editor at a national magazine told me, "Give me a lead like that every time, and I'll keep you busy." And she did. That's the power of an exciting lead—not only does it grab your readers' attention, it makes the writing process more fun for you.

@          @          @

## EXCITING TO WRITE = EXCITING TO READ

Earlier, I shared ideas for leads—tell a story, make an observation (like I did above), use a quote, ask a question. But I also appreciate how, after writing eight documents in a week, it can be challenging to come up with something fresh. When that happens, try this creativity boost:

Pick up the *New York Times* or *The New Yorker* (or your favorites) and review the leads. Without fail, I find all kinds of examples of business and scientific information shared with remarkable humor, suspense, and vivacity.

Maybe the author used an anecdote from someone's life. Or compared today's situation to what it was like 50 years ago. Or one of my favorites—a hint of a problem (or solution) that you have to keep reading to discover. There's nothing wrong with this creativity boost—nothing even remotely related to plagiarism or laziness. Just a fun way to remind yourself of all the storytelling techniques available to you.

### All in good time

Now, let's discuss *when* to write your lead. Read three books on writing, and you'll likely read three different opinions. Common wisdom holds that you don't have to write it when you start the document. Maybe you won't know your lead till the piece is finished, or maybe you'll lead with something just to prime your pump and improve it later.

That's all good advice—if it works for you. It doesn't for me. Early on, I tried to let the lead come to me as I wrote the article, but it never arrived! I was sure I was doing something wrong, wasting time as I waited for my lead before proceeding to write. Finally, after a few months of that, I gave up trying to follow someone else's rules. I *have* to write my lead before I can go ahead with the story. I need my lead from the beginning because it serves as the compass that keeps my story headed in the right direction. But that's me. This is your journey. Work with the method that lets your writing flow. And trust your instincts (more on that later).

### @ Six extras for excitement

Take time to write better, and someone at the top will notice. Guaranteed. That's true in part because writing leads us to those brilliant ideas we discussed earlier and helps us work them out in more detail. Text messaging? That's just top-of-the-head stuff. Ditto most e-mails. Take a little more time, edit one extra round, and get beyond the obvious.

Besides, why be like everyone else? Too often we read reports or proposals that basically say, "We're great, we have the solution, trust us." Be uncommon and catch your readers' interest (including bosses, clients, customers).

Once your lead jump-starts your writing, try these six techniques to add polish and pizzazz.

## 1. Similes

These figures of speech compare two unlike things, usually introduced by *like* or *as*.

@ *His work becomes even more remarkable when you realize that Brush is self-taught, though that's like saying Albert Einstein taught himself relativity one day on a moving train.* (Lapidary Journal)

@ *These days, looking into employment trends and employee attitudes is like gazing into a crystal ball crafted by Dale Chihuly: everything swirls in one direction, then dramatically shifts in another.* (NICHE)

@ *And like the glaciers that carved the Upper Peninsula's watery boundaries—lakes Superior, Huron and Michigan—the snow and solitude leave their mark on the dozens of artists who live here.* (AmericanStyle)

Similes paint a picture and draw readers into your letter or report, proposal or blog. They're especially good at taking complex ideas and making them easier to understand. I used this technique earlier when I said writing was like picking blackberries or making bread. I also used similes to share information I had learned from Jonah Lehrer's article in *The New Yorker*, "The Eureka Hunt" (comparing two parts of the brain to a short-order cook and an executive chef). In that same article, one of the researchers refers to studies that illustrated how the prefrontal cortex was more than a collector of information.

> *Instead, it was like the conductor of an orchestra, waving its baton and directing the players.* (Page 45)

When you're writing a complex proposal or you'd like your readers to imagine a pleasant outcome (using your product, hiring you for the job, etc.), try crafting a simile. Start by getting clear on what you want to convey; then think of how your subject matter is similar to something your readers will quickly understand. Maybe you're explaining an important step the board must take. "This next step is like oxygen to the project; it will sustain the progress we've made as well as our future plans."

Or perhaps you're introducing a new policy vital to your company's growth. "XYZ is like a personal trainer, building our company's stamina while reducing the effects of our merger."

## 2. Alliteration

Alliteration is the lyrical repetition of initial consonant sounds in two or more neighboring words or syllables (as *w*ild and *w*oolly, *thr*eatening *thr*ongs). It adds interest and develops rhythm. For example:

> *By its nature, art furniture is a loosely structured movement, a sort of Chippendale-meets-Chip 'n' Dale style that mixes tradition and whimsy, function and fun.* (AmericanStyle)

Alliteration requires only that phonetics match, not initial first letters. For example, wild one and fat Phoenicians are alliterative.

Use alliteration and your blogs and reports will stand out. So will you. People will admire your ability to express yourself.

### 3. Cool clichés and plays on words.

Catch readers' attention with a cliché or phrase made fresh for your topic. Typically, clichés are catchy—but trite. Change them just enough to grab attention—and make people smile. (And who won't think kindly of someone who makes them smile at work?)

*1. Best suite in the house* (in an ad for a condominium).

*2. He learned it the soft way* (a  legendary frozen custard entrepreneur).

*3. Familiarity breeds unkempt, which is exactly what happens when your grammatical slips are showing* (how poor writing gives us a bad image).

*4. Art-to-art talk* (an art symposium).

### 4. Famous quotes

*"Anybody can become angry—that is easy. But to be angry with the right person, and to the right degree, and at the right time, and for the right purpose, and in the right way—that is not within everybody's power and is not easy."*

Aristotle (used at the beginning of an article on anger in the workplace.)

Famous quotes deliver a boost in credibility. Use them judiciously, though, and don't depend on famous people to make your point. You want people to think you're the smart one—not Aristotle! You can find a slew of famous quotes on the Web. Just type in your key words and look for a quote that illustrates your point.

## 5. Vivid verbs

When I edit clients' work, my biggest—and most rewarding—task is to replace "to be" verbs with something more exciting. Just a few strong verbs can add a lot of energy. Of course, sometimes nothing works better than "is," "are" or "was." You can't have every verb a zinger; too many can actually distract from your message. But we overuse the "to be" verb. Consider these before and after examples.

(Dull)    He was the first person to do that.
(Vivid)   He created that.

(Dull)    She is very tall.
(Vivid)   She looms over the crowd.

(Dull)    The waistband is tight.
(Vivid)   The waistband pinches.

(Dull)    The file is full of paper.
(Vivid)   The file bulges with paper.

(Dull)    The boss's remark was hurtful.
(Vivid)   The boss's remark stung.

As you review your work, look for chances to ratchet up your prose. Add color and action with verbs such as:

- abandon, achieve, accommodate, aggravate
- brandish, carve, celebrate, collaborate
- demand, devote, discover, encourage, establish
- festoon, fracture, galvanize, generate, honor, implement, invest
- kick, launch, leer, maintain, neutralize
- organize, originate, oppress, pout, prove, ravage, reveal, rummage
- scare, shout, simper, stabilize, sustain, swarm
- target, taunt, unfettered, uphold, wither, wilt

## 6. Variety of sentence structures

Long sentences. Short sentences. Complex and incomplete. Just as a salad gets better with more texture—diced avocado, chunky tomatoes, and thinly sliced cucumber—a good paragraph needs a variety of sentence structures. Vary the length for impact. After a long explanation, add punch with a short or even incomplete sentence. It works! Some grammarians pull their hair out over incomplete sentences, but so what? They add verve and break the monotony. Next time you have to write a long proposal or report, give your readers a break. Look for places where you can add variety by turning one long sentence into two. Add punch with a short sentence. Sneak in an incomplete sentence or two. Be bold! Your results will be bold too.

# Chapter Nine|Show, don't tell

**W**hen I moved to Washington, D.C., a new world of writing opportunities opened for me. Hundreds of associations (many publishing their own magazines) are headquartered there, and dozens of newspapers and journals need freelance writers to fill their broadsheets and tabloids. For the first time in my career, I found that some stories I wrote were covered by two or three publications, which let me see how other writers handled the same topic. It wasn't always pleasant.

Like the time I wrote about the Smithsonian Craft Show, arguably the best craft exhibition in America. Ever since the Campbell Folk School, I've been passionate about handmade objects and the people who make them, so I was delighted with the assignment.

Later, I was drinking coffee and reading the *Washington Post* when I noticed an article on the same event. As I made my way down the first column, my stomach churned. By the end of the article, I felt sick.

I realized that the piece I'd written was full of breathless pronouncements and assumptions *telling* the readers how great everything was. While I gushed about the great artists who were slated to exhibit, the *Post*'s writer told stories about the artists and created reader-to-artist connections.

My piece was lame. But all we can do is to keep learning. I saved that *Post* article to make sure I did.

@        @        @

## TELLING TALES FOR FUN AND PROFIT

Observation is one of the best ways to develop stories. Pay attention to anecdotes in everyday life—and write them down. (Your memory really isn't as good as you think.) As a reporter, I've honed the skills of looking and listening. I eavesdrop at restaurants and on buses (and hear the most amazing things). One of my favorite observations took place on the highest summit in Georgia, Brasstown Bald (4,784 feet). Ten years later, I used their exchange for a lead in an article about wildflowers.

*Two women walking in the woods stopped to investigate a shock of red against the muted forest floor.*

*"What's that?" one asked.*

*"Oh, nothing," the other said. "Just an old wildflower."*

*I overheard this exchange almost 20 years ago, but I still can't believe my ears. They stood before petals of red, dew-dotted emerald leaves, pistils laden with gold, fragrance as sweet as the senses can register—a flower that had returned year after year through too much rain and too little, through winter's cold and summer's heat. And they dissed it?*

Listen to what your customers, employees, bosses—whomever you're writing to—have to say. Eavesdrop. Ask questions. What do they like? What would make their lives easier? In a perfect world, what do they hope you can deliver? Shape your documents to respond to their needs. Remember that our biggest task in business writing is to write to our reader, not just dump our information on them.

Stories increase your readers' ability to grasp your information. Instead of deadly diatribes or boring Power-Points, share stories, scenarios, situations, and case studies. Consider how fiction writers tell stories: When the hero faces danger, rather than writing, "She's scared," they write about her sweating forehead and hands, the gun slipping from her grip. They show rather than tell.

Why not bring the same verve to business writing? Whatever you're writing—reports, sales letter, Web content, blogs, newsletter article, proposals, training manuals—share a story that will conjure some emotion from your readers. A bad situation you can fix. A recurring problem your company can solve. Stir up a little pain, and your readers will begin to identify with you as the solution.

Consider this letter to business owners, informing them of the need to have their water heaters inspected. No one enjoys learning about another government requirement, but you can soften the blow with a story.

**Before**

> *The purpose of the Springfield Boiler and Pressure Code No. 4545 is to establish and provide minimum standards for the protection of public health, safety and property by regulating and controlling the quality, location and installation of boilers, pressure vessels and their appurtenances within the City of Springfield.*
>
> *It is a state and city ordinance requirement that water heaters located in places of public assembly be inspected annually and Certificates of Inspection issued. The fee for an annual inspection and certificate is $37.65 per water heater...*

What might keep the reader from tossing this in the trash? A story. Besides, when people understand a situation, they can be remarkably cooperative.

**After**

> *Last year, faulty water heaters injured hundreds of children and adults. More than 50 businesses in our area suffered damages—and lawsuits— when water heaters exploded. None of this had to happen.*
>
> *That's why the City of Springfield takes its job of inspecting water heaters so seriously. The sole purpose of our Boiler and Pressure Code*

*is to regulate and control the quality, location, and installation of boilers, pressure vessels, and other related equipment within the city.*

*The City of Springfield requires that water heaters located in places of public assembly be inspected annually and Certificates of Inspection issued. (The state has similar requirements.) The fee for an annual inspection and certificate is only $37.65 per water heater.*

## @ Evocative descriptions

Fiction writers draw us into their stories by awakening our senses. You can too. If you're writing a report about a problem, for example, grab your readers' attention by showing how people typically react to the situation. Are their hands shaking as they try a complicated device? Are they frowning, muttering under their breath, or scratching their heads? Is the room filled with an unmistakable sense of dread?

Or, after you've implemented some changes, maybe they feel proud, energized, relaxed. Their eyes light up as they understand what to do next, or they let out a soft sigh of relief. The energy in the room feels electric.

Put yourself in the situation and imagine it fully—the feelings, smells, tastes, sounds, and sights. Not all senses are always appropriate, but pick a few to trigger your readers' emotions and immerse them in your message. This technique works especially well in letters, reports, articles, Web copy, and blogs.

@ **Benefits and results instead of features and facts**

Now, try using descriptive stories when writing about benefits and results. For example, rather than telling your readers that your business provides excellent marketing advice, show them with the experience of a satisfied customer:

> *As Tracy Mitchell sealed the envelopes stuffed with 20 new invoices, tears streamed down her face. Tears of joy. A few months ago, she was about to close her doors. With some solid advice from XYZ Company—and a willingness to implement change—she's back in the black.*

Okay, not Hemingway, but see how you can introduce readers to what you do through a descriptive story?

Stories work especially well in sales materials and training manuals. Too often, these documents can be deadly boring, which means all too often they go unread. Use real-life situations and what-if scenarios to engage your readers' imagination. We're a storytelling culture, and we like to learn by example—rather than lecture. That's why stories make our messages stick. How else can you explain remembering stories round the campfire decades later?

@ **Cover stories get the job done**

Applying for a job you really want? Try writing stories rather than trite phrases like "To Whom It May Concern" or "This letter is in regards to your ad..." People reading these letters are already bored with the reams of pablum they have to read, do you really want to make them comatose?

I don't know why people present themselves that way. It's like wearing a dreary brown suit to an interview (if you ever get that far). Yet, every day I see how people resist being creative when introducing themselves to a new company.

Why?

Fear again. I often see it in clients' eyes when I tell them to be uncommon. Not weird—interesting. Not reckless—creative.

"You expect me to write something different?" they ask, gulping.

"Well, are you different from the other candidates? Are you the best choice?" I ask.

"Yes," they answer with great confidence.

"Okay, then *show* it."

A good story about what you've accomplished *shows* them why you're the best candidate. It also shows you've got a head on your shoulders.

Sadly, most don't listen. That's a real shame, because resume reviewers enjoy reading something different.

Jennifer Dupper, a recruiter for Starbucks in Seattle, Washington, says she takes special notice of candidates with good writing skills.

> *"A well-written cover letter makes such a positive difference!" she says. "When I'm screening an inbox full of applications and come across an interesting cover letter, I'm not only excited to view the resume, but more likely to contact the candidate—even when their experience may be lacking some of the necessary requirements of the position they are seeking."*

With that in mind, compare these examples.

**Before**

> *Please accept this letter and accompanying resume in application for the XYZ Director position advertised in the Boise Bulletin. As the current executive director of ABC Imports in Washington and Oregon, I have the skills required, and I'd like to remain in this region.*
>
> *In my current role, I have utilized the essential functions found in the job descriptions. This includes .... [z-z-z-z-z-z-z-z]*

**After**

> *I believe the best way to convey my qual-ifications for the XYZ director position is through an example from my tenure as*

*executive director of ABC Imports. Last April, I was having lunch with a manager of one of our divisions. He's good at his job, and we've enjoyed working together. So, I was surprised when he suddenly grew angry. He told me he resented the way headquarters was telling him how to run his division.*

*I took a deep breath and reminded myself this man was frustrated, maybe even a little scared. He needed our help, even though he couldn't admit it to himself.*

*Today, that situation has changed dramatically, and this manager is back on track...*
*[Highlights of relevant experience follow.]*

When you need to write a cover letter, think of a personal story that *shows* why you're the best, then tell about it in relation to the job specifications. Your results may well be the opposite of those doled out by that curmudgeon on "The Apprentice." Instead, you'll hear, "You're hired!"

# Chapter Ten | Less is more

**A** few years ago, when I was new to Seattle, I attended a lot of networking events as I tried to find my place there. I attended a picnic sponsored by a local editors association, and as we crunched our carrot sticks and gulped our deviled eggs, the conversation turned to semicolons and the misuse of parentheses. Later, a heated discussion ensued over the use of "that'" and "which." I admit I've enjoyed feeling smug a time or two when I knew the difference between compose and comprise or further and farther, but honestly, that's all so small-minded. Sure, it's important to know grammar, but good writing is about more substantive stuff:

the excitement your lead generates, the rhythm you've created with just the right words, the pacing of your story, and your presentation of the facts.

I know plenty of people who think editing is boring and difficult. But look at it this way: You've finished the hard part—the dreadful first draft—and now you can start the creative part. Editing is your chance to add interesting examples, turn a phrase or two, and cut the flab. This is the stage where you can really excel.

In case you're still thinking that you shouldn't *need* to edit, consider E. B. White. He's best known for his children's books *Charlotte's Web* and *Stuart Little*, but he also wrote essays for the *The New Yorker*. The first time I read them, I was convinced he just jotted them down while sitting on the front porch of his farmhouse in Maine. Here's the truth: It took him 20 to 25 edits to get that warm, conversational tone—and even then he didn't think they were good enough. These essays are some of the best writing I've ever read. So, when I'm struggling with a piece, I remind myself that if E. B. White had to edit 25 times, there's no shame in my having to do that too.

@          @          @

## GOOD WRITING IS REALLY GOOD EDITING

Right about now, if you were sitting in one of my seminars, you'd see several people raising their hands, brows furrowed. They're complaining that this much editing will take too long. Not true. Instead of spending 30 minutes in one fell swoop, try 10 minutes at three different times. This saves time because our brains are sharper in shorter sprints. After a break, it will help you spot more things to improve. (I'm not sure why, maybe our brains get bored, too, with the longer sessions.) Three short sessions won't take any more of your time, but the results are guaranteed to be sharper.

And besides, if extra editing gets you better results, isn't that worth it?

One of the most important steps in the writing process is knowing when to welcome back your OE (ornery editor). We've talked about not letting him come in too soon, like the neighbor who rings your doorbell on Friday for the party you're throwing on Saturday. Not a bad person, just in the right place at the wrong time. But come Saturday, your OE can be your best friend. Like those times you're feeling self-satisfied and he disagrees. Listen to him *now* because he's almost always right in this situation.

### @ Short cuts to success

My students and clients often ask me what they're supposed to look for when they edit. Their OE is making them uncomfortable, they know they need to do something, but what? Obviously, start by cutting words and catching typos, but editing is so much more than that. It's about transforming choppy copy with funky flow into something smooth and compelling. When I'm editing, I look for six key qualities: conversational, clear, concise, creative, constructive, and complete.

## 1. Conversational (engaging)

If you want people to read your documents, make them open and friendly. Too often our writing is full of corporatespeak. Forget sounding august, the way I did back in the day. Nothing short of poor grammar makes a writer sound less professional than a studied aloofness. Relax. Tell a good story. No one wants to be lectured. And like any good conversation, don't write a monologue—get your readers involved. Pretend you're having a conversation with your target-audience members. Ask them questions, listen to their answers. In other words, have a conversation.

### Before

*The purpose of this letter is to inform you that the communications endeavor we planned to originate in the month of March unfortunately will be postponed until later inasmuch as the necessary components have been delayed until further notice. We will keep you apprised of the pending date.*

**After**

> *We regret that the communications program planned for March has been postponed. You will receive an announcement when we re-launch the program.*

## 2. Clear (avoid jargon)

Cut the mumbo-jumbo when you can. Sometimes jargon works. If your audience is comprised solely of your peers, it's okay to use the language of your trade. Also, today certain acronyms have become the norm—FBI, PPO, and ASAP. Most terms, though, should be introduced the first time with the spelled-out version followed by the acronym in parentheses: Association for Creative Business Writing (AFCBW) or American Society of Journalists and Authors (ASJA). From then on, you may use only the acronym. Other pointers to keep in mind as you edit:

- Avoid archaic language—incumbent on, betwixt, behoove, derring-do.

- Skip exaggeration or too-strong descriptions:
  (No) This is a disaster. (Yes) We have a problem.

- Cut out public-relations language:
  (No) The committee debated the issue and eventually determined that the employees needed to be hydrated.
  (Yes) The committee approved the water cooler.

- Lose the legalese. Unless you're a lawyer, avoid: pursuant to, be advised that, herein, heretofore, etc. And even if you have Esq. after your name, you don't have license to write convoluted communications.

**Before**

> *The basic fundamentals of the AMA course are herewith enclosed. Important essentials of such a campaign—from the beginning to the final ending—are included, with particular spotlight on the hidden pitfalls that can be generated over an extended period of time.*

**After**

> *The fundamentals of the American Marketing Association (AMA) course are enclosed. This course features the essential steps in a marketing campaign—from start to finish—with emphasis on the pitfalls of a long campaign.*

### 3. Concise (edit and edit again)

Cutting out words, hard as they were to conjure in the first place, is one of the best ways you can improve your writing. Too often, we've used three words when one would do. Think of all those extra words as the love handles of writing and get in shape.

For example, change, "When I heard someone behind me, my heart began to beat faster and I began to walk very fast" to "When I heard someone behind me, my heart raced and I began to run." See how these cuts and corrections quicken the pace and add intrigue?

Next, get rid of most of your adjectives and adverbs. It's an easy trap to fall into—stringing together several adjectives to make sure you got the point across when one strong word would do it best. Cut out flabby descriptions and weak (or virtually synonymous) adjectives. Of course, concise does not mean brief. Keep every word necessary for the readers' understanding.

## Before

*It is very important that communication with all individuals involved in this process be frequent and continuous.*

## After

*Communicate often with everyone involved.*
*or*
*Keep everyone informed throughout the process.*

More concise tips:

@ Redundant words make your writing sloppy: past history, unwanted trespassers, postpone until later, completely destroyed, hidden pitfalls, month of April.

@ Cut out "very" whenever possible. Believe it or not, your copy is usually stronger without it.

@ Avoid using long words when short ones will do. When you try to impress with your extensive vocabulary, it usually backfires.

@ Similarly, don't use *utilize* for *use*, *institute* for *adopt*, or *on a regular basis* for *routinely*.

@ Avoid run-on sentences. Use a period or a semicolon to divide thoughts; or use a conjunction (or, and, but, if, because, as) after each one to tie like thoughts together. (But don't join unlike thoughts—simply put a period at the end of each sentence.)

**Before:**

*"But, it still works!"*

*This is a very common remark from those who have the responsibility of maintaining a company's reliance on computer technology. With a primary focus on maintaining profitability while keeping costs down many times the reliance upon computer hardware and software technology is overlooked. The common thinking is, "If it ain't broke, don't fix it!" It is amazing how many companies take this approach, while not realizing that their once dependable infrastructure of technology is on the verge of a catastrophic meltdown!*

**After**

*"But, it still works!"*

*We often hear this remark from people who maintain their company's computer technology. They're working hard, keeping an eye on profitability—so sometimes they overlook the importance of upgrading computer hardware and software technology.*

*In other words, "If it ain't broke, don't fix it."*

*We're writing to show you how important—and economical—it is to keep your once-dependable infrastructure from a catastrophic melt-down.*

## 4. Creative (attention-getting)

This step is my favorite. Creative business writing can include all kinds of techniques, some borrowed from fiction writing, to keep readers engaged.

@ Boring introductory clauses using "there" and "it" plus "to-be" verbs are often just lazy writing. Look out for these as you edit, and make them more active.

(Boring) There are many ways to organize a document.

(Interesting) Start documents with a story, a quote, or a question.

(Boring)    It is so cold in the office.

(Interesting) I'm freezing!

@ Direct quotes and dialogue add veracity and verve. Depending on the document, you may not be able to share your opinion, but you can let others speak freely. This works especially well in internal documents where you can quote the CEO or VP of Sales in order to give your proposal or memo added oomph from upstairs.

@ Foreshadowing and flashbacks add intrigue to reports and proposals. Create drama and tension by telling the story in a certain order, withholding information until key points. For example, when you're introducing a new policy, start with what will happen if the policy *isn't* adopted. "Next year, five key accounts could be in the hands of ABC. We can start today to make sure that doesn't happen, but only if we..."

@ Stories draw in your readers. (Chapter Nine)

@ Six Extras for Excitement (Chapter Eight) all add spice to your writing.

## Before

*Dear Alex, (head of a PR firm)*

*Would you like your employees to get better results from their writing? I offer one-on-one coaching to help your employees develop a clear, creative style and brush up on their writing skills. It often takes only a few sessions to show them how to make a big difference...*

## After

*Dear Alex,*

*You probably know someone like Carole. After 15 years in commercial real estate, she's putting her expertise to work in a fresh way—as a senior account executive for a leading PR agency. Her extensive knowledge is helping the agency attract and retain key accounts.*

*Trouble is, she doesn't write well. She brings plenty of professional expertise but little writing know-how.*

### Coaching for excellence

*Does your agency have a Carole or two? I offer one-on-one coaching to help them develop a clear, creative style and brush up on their writing skills. It often takes only a few sessions to show them how to make a big difference...*

## 5. Constructive

Be clear on your purpose and your audience. Make sure your tone offers encouragement whenever possible and avoids negative words. Even a reprimand can have a constructive tone. Organize it so the bad news is sandwiched between positive comments (Chapter One, Bad News Burrito).

### Before

*John:*

*The last report you sent in wasn't on time or accurate. At Acme Sales, our expectations are high. We expect staff to respond to deadlines responsibly and accurately. I don't have time to correct your work. It goes without saying that we expect better next time.*

### After

*Dear John:*

*Over the past year, I've watched you grow into an excellent salesman. Maybe that's why I was disappointed with your last report. It was late, and I found several inaccuracies.*

*We have high standards at Acme Sales. I want*

*to go over this report with you so that you know
what I expect. You've got a lot of potential, and
I know you can get this right.*

*Let me know your schedule this week so we can
get together.*

## 6. Complete

Did you say everything you need to say? Here again,
a little time away from the document helps. Step back,
then check and double-check to make sure you say it all.
Now proofread once more for punctuation and grammar
mistakes.

The following e-mail memo lacks key components
such as a compelling lead and closing (including
contact information)—not to mention how offensive it is.
How could he have addressed this sensitive topic more
thoughtfully?

## Before

### *Subject line: Breast Cancer Awareness Month*

*In light of Breast Cancer Awareness Month,
First Met has developed a financial seminar to
bring women together. It will be a fun evening
of learning and sharing of financial knowledge
and experience with other women while making
new friends. First Met will make a financial
donation to breast cancer research for each
attendee. So, please bring your friends. We'll
have wine, cheese, and hors d' oeuvres. Please*

Less is more

*RSVP to tinasmith@finsvvc.com at your earliest convenience as space is limited. Please mention that I invited you!! -Jeremy*

**After**

### Subject line: Financial seminar to benefit breast cancer research

*Hello everyone,*

*In support of Breast Cancer Awareness Month, First Met is offering a financial seminar for women. We will make a financial donation to breast cancer research for each attendee, so please bring your friends.*

### Food for thought

*We've planned a fun evening of sharing financial knowledge and experiences. We'll also have a good selection of wine, cheese, and hors d'oeuvres.*

### RSVP

*Please RSVP to tinasmith@finsvvc.com at your earliest convenience—and please mention I invited you. This lively evening not only features financial information—it represents an important step toward your financial security and peace of mind.*

*Thanks, and I look forward to seeing you again, Jeremy Johnson, Financial Planner*
*First Met, 222.899.0999*

## @ Lose your darlings

It's hard to edit our *bon mots* because we think they're so clever. Sometimes they are. Often they're not. I see a lot of darlings in promotional copy. We want to say something fresh, not the same old way, but we get carried away and end up with confusing babble. Consider this one:

*Imagine, then, relaxing on our beautiful ship in Comstock Bay. Nothing but the sounds of the seagulls and the water slapping the shore. Then step inside to enjoy a romantic dinner and dance to your favorite music. A smiling face serving your favorite drink.*

If a smiling face served me a drink, I'd run screaming. Courteous staff with smiling faces, okay, but I've never seen (and I hope I never do) a smiling face serving anything.

To make matters worse, we often fall in love with what we've written. We convince ourselves that it's poetic or worse, brilliant. But we've just created a monster (a.k.a., our darlings).

*Our ship is an oasis in time allowing you to relax, refresh, and recharge your soul. This romantic trip is just around the corner. One that can lift the spirits and refreshen the mind.*

Hmmm, corners at sea? I don't think so. And I guess if we refresh in the first sentence, naturally we would refreshen in the third one, though Daniel Webster doesn't agree.

# Chapter Eleven | Time out!

**A** few years ago, I had the privilege of interviewing Jeffery Robinson, whose career as a criminal defense lawyer was shaped by the Civil Rights Movement he witnessed firsthand as a boy in Memphis, Tennessee. He is a kind, courteous, and caring person, and I wanted to do him justice. I enjoyed working on his profile, but I also enjoyed crossing it off my to-do list when I finished. Trouble was, I wasn't finished. I *thought* I was, but when I started squirming uncomfortably in my chair (a sure signal from my ornery editor), I asked an editor friend to look it over. She came back with the dreaded words, "You're not done."

Of course, I knew that, deep down. Having one less thing to do was so tantalizing. But we need to resist this tempation, and I finally grasped this while finishing— really finishing—Jeffery Robinson's story. The final version, the one I completed after my friend's warning, was so much better. In fact, one paragraph even drew praise from my editor. (A rare commodity—they usually only mention what's wrong.)

Originally, that paragraph contained some prosaic comment like, "Robinson has amassed an impressive list of awards." (No wonder my friend said I wasn't done!) I tried all kinds of different approaches, but I couldn't come up with anything better. I gave up and took a nap. When I awoke 15 minutes later, this phrase immediately flowed through my head: "If awards were legal tender, Robinson could forget about billable hours."

Where did that come from? I'm not sure, but I think that my executive chef played a part. I think she was cooking up ideas before and during my nap and sent them to my short-order cook (conscious brain) when I awoke. These gems have little to do with talent and everything to do with respect for the unknown, as well as patience and practice. That means giving your writing the time it deserves. Everyone complains about not having enough time, but how are you spending the time you do have?

We never really learned how to write well in school. Like my scratch-it-off-the-list mentality, we just want to get our writing done. But good writing doesn't work that way. Sure, get your first draft done fast, but then spend the rest of your time editing, resting, and editing some more. Who knows what will come out of that fabulous brain of yours? Ask your executive chef to join you while you walk, sleep, daydream, or sip coffee. It's like having a personal writing coach.

@          @          @

## Take a break

My friend Virginia McCullough, writing coach and author, has more than 100 books to her credit, many of which she wrote and edited longhand in her Chicago neighborhood coffee shop. She's living proof that a change of scene is good for waking up your creativity. If you can, get out of the office, go somewhere unfamiliar, order a cup of coffee, and watch your results improve. Get in a dreamy state and open the conduit between your executive chef and inner short-order cook. It may take a little extra time, but it's fun. You'll wake up your brain and feel more motivated (way more than if you stay stuck in your cubicle or office). Take the time to do it right. Remember, bad writers just stopped too soon.

This chapter is short so that you can take a break. Go to a diner, get in the tub—just about anywhere—to loosen up your brain. And while you're at it, make something you've written even better.

*RSVP to tinasmith@finsvvc.com at your earliest convenience as space is limited. Please mention that I invited you!! -Jeremy*

**After**

### Subject line: Financial seminar to benefit breast cancer research

*Hello everyone,*

*In support of Breast Cancer Awareness Month, First Met is offering a financial seminar for women. We will make a financial donation to breast cancer research for each attendee, so please bring your friends.*

### Food for thought
*We've planned a fun evening of sharing financial knowledge and experiences. We'll also have a good selection of wine, cheese, and hors d'oeuvres.*

### RSVP
*Please RSVP to tinasmith@finsvvc.com at your earliest convenience—and please mention I invited you. This lively evening not only features financial information—it represents an important step toward your financial security and peace of mind.*

*Thanks, and I look forward to seeing you again, Jeremy Johnson, Financial Planner First Met, 222.899.0999*

### @ Lose your darlings

It's hard to edit our *bon mots* because we think they're so clever. Sometimes they are. Often they're not. I see a lot of darlings in promotional copy. We want to say something fresh, not the same old way, but we get carried away and end up with confusing babble. Consider this one:

> *Imagine, then, relaxing on our beautiful ship in Comstock Bay. Nothing but the sounds of the seagulls and the water slapping the shore. Then step inside to enjoy a romantic dinner and dance to your favorite music. A smiling face serving your favorite drink.*

If a smiling face served me a drink, I'd run screaming. Courteous staff with smiling faces, okay, but I've never seen (and I hope I never do) a smiling face serving anything.

To make matters worse, we often fall in love with what we've written. We convince ourselves that it's poetic or worse, brilliant. But we've just created a monster (a.k.a., our darlings).

> *Our ship is an oasis in time allowing you to relax, refresh, and recharge your soul. This romantic trip is just around the corner. One that can lift the spirits and refreshen the mind.*

Hmmm, corners at sea? I don't think so. And I guess if we refresh in the first sentence, naturally we would refreshen in the third one, though Daniel Webster doesn't agree.

Let your darlings go. If you feel yourself digging in your heels to keep something cute, it probably needs to go. (Your OE is nudging you to hit "delete." This is the perfect time to listen to him.) When you let your copy rest and allow time for clear-headed review, you'll usually find they're not so darling after all.

### @ Find a friend

Finally, find an editing buddy so you can review each other's work. For important projects, it's too iffy to review your own work—your brain skips over or fills in blanks because it already knows what you're trying to say.

# Chapter Twelve | When good advice goes bad

**B**y the time I was in kindergarten, I'd already been told hundreds of times not to get in the car with strange men. Good thing, too, because one crisp autumn morning, a creepy guy pulled up in a battered Ford Galaxy, rolled down his window, and told me my coat was pretty. When he asked me to get in his car so he could get a closer look at the wooden buttons, my mother's warning went off like sirens. "Oh no you don't," I shouted, already halfway up the hill toward home.

Thirty years later, I was on a highway just after midnight when my car broke down during a snow storm. I turned that key a dozen times, but the starter just groaned. Nothing I could do but start walking. After half a mile, frozen and scared, I felt a gigantic truck barrel past. Then I saw its backup lights and brake lights and two doors opening. Two burly guys jumped out dressed in camo. As they started toward me, my mother's warning screamed again.

One of them began waving his arms like a semaphore, shouting in a deep Southern accent, "Do not be afraid, we are here to help you." And they were. They escorted me to their truck—a chicken-manure hauler!—and lifted me into the cab, where I sat perched halfway on one man's lap and painfully close to third gear. We rumbled along, and pretty soon I was home, safe and warm.

What does this have to do with writing? Sometimes you need to listen to the advice people offer—and sometimes you need to ignore them (just like you need to do with your ornery editor). These days, everyone's a writer, clicking away at computers and Blackberries. A fair number of them seem predisposed to tell you what they think, whether you want their advice or not. But none of them knows what you're trying to express. You may need to run away from them and say to yourself, "Oh, no you don't!"

Other times, don't be too cautious to accept help. Swallow your pride and admit that you've got some learning to do. Listen. Look things up. Take classes. You'll find a wealth of them online, or better yet, find a community of writers and meet face-to-face. Oh, and buy a dictionary. Sure, it's easy to check a word online, but you only get that one word. When you open a hard-copy dictionary, you might see "isobars" on your way to "irrevocable." Or "quetzal" just above "queue." No telling when that will come in handy.

And listen to your instincts. If you trust the source, like I did my good-hearted truck drivers, go with them. Let them help. If you don't, tell them to get lost. It's not easy to tell the difference. Sometimes I've wondered if I've ever turned down help that would have made my life easier. I doubt it. I like my instincts and intuition. I hope you get to know yours and respect them too.

@          @          @

**ELEVEN MORE WAYS TO ACHIEVE POWERFUL WRITING**
**—FASTER, STRONGER, BETTER.**

**1. Don't skimp on planning and organizing.**
Time spent in preparation to write actually saves time in the long run.

**2. Write a Velcro lead**. Grab the readers' attention and don't let go.

**3. Vary the Pace.** Use different sentence structures—from long to short, complex to incomplete. Add variety to engage your readers.

**4. Take a walk**. Then edit again. Let a document rest while you take a short walk or a long lunch. You'll come back fresher and better able to spot necessary changes.

**5. Check your vitality dipstick.** Once you've edited a time or two, go back and look for ways to make it more interesting. Use vivid verbs, similes, metaphors, alliteration. Think of inventive ways to enliven the mundane and explain technical information.

**6. Make pages easy to read.** Use headlines, subheads, pull quotes, white spaces, bullets, numbers, and graphics to help readers *want* to read your writing.

**7. Tie it all together.** Pack a real punch at the end to keep the reader thinking about your message.

**8. Print & Proofread.** Print it out—for some reason, we catch more mistakes in hard copy than on a computer screen. Besides typos and misspellings, look for goofs such as run-on sentences, verbs with the wrong tenses, pronouns/verbs that don't agree, passive voice, and negative wording. At work, find a proofreading buddy—and proof one another's documents.

**9. Read aloud for flow.** Cadence matters. Your readers will hear your words in their heads, so read out loud and listen for what they'll hear. This is a great way to catch fuzzy wording and awkward phrasing.

**10. Sleep on it.** Rest and let your writing rest. Then edit and proof again with fresh insights.

**11. Read voraciously.** My favorite way of writing better. You might want to pay attention to how different authors introduce concepts and organize material. Or you might want to just have fun. Either way, your writing will improve.

# Final thoughts | The Orchard Trap

**W**e've covered a lot of territory, but I want to share one more tip, something I call The Orchard Trap.

When I lived on my farm, I had a large pasture near my front porch. Many evenings we sat there, rocking and talking about what a great orchard that would make. I imagined all the applesauce I could put by, the pies I could bake. We thought about pears, too, and even peaches. Years later, by the time I moved away, it was still a pasture in serious need of mowing. The enormity of plowing it, buying all those trees, and planting an orchard had overwhelmed me.

Instead, I wish I had planted one tree a year. By the time I left, I would have had an orchard, some of the trees already heavy with fruit. I would have had jars of applesauce in my cellar and a pie or two under my belt.

**Start small, grow big**

The Orchard Trap affects a lot of my clients. They know how important it is to write regularly, and they make big plans to write every day. That's an honorable notion and definitely one of the best ways to become a good writer. But sometimes, given their busy schedules, such a big commitment can actually keep them from writing much at all. Sure enough, by our next session, they're embarrassed and even discouraged because they wrote every day for three, maybe four days, but then missed a few days and decided their plan wouldn't work after all. Just like those New Year's resolutions to give up sugar that are abandoned after the first hot fudge sundae. Or the exercise routine. Or, or...we have all kinds of traps that set us up to fail.

Instead, why not just start writing? No big plans. If you don't write for a few days, so what? Start writing again. And again. And again. That's what's worked for me for more than 25 years. I've interviewed amazing unsung heroes and a celebrity or two. I've learned a lot about how organizations work and why people do crazy things. I'm still not published in *The New Yorker*, but you know, that doesn't matter to me anymore. Maybe someday I will be. Or not. The point is that I still love to write and that I've never written anything half-heartedly. Some of it seems amateurish to me now, but it was the best I could create at the time. Gradually I improved as I studied and learned and compared and developed my own personal tool kit of everything I'd learned along the way.

And now, as a business writing coach, I get to pass it all along to you. Like that O at the end of the inverted pyramid, it feels as though everything has come full circle.

@          @          @

# Want to learn more? Check out these easy ways to improve your business writing

- **Free Editing for Success Checklist**: Would you like a free tool to help you edit like a pro? Contact me at www.LyndaMcDaniel.com for your copy of this handy list.

- **Coaching**: Do you want to develop a clear, creative style to advance your career? My one-on-one coaching starts with a personal assessment and focuses on areas that *you* need to improve. It often takes only a few sessions to make a big difference. www.LyndaMcDaniel.com/Coaching.asp

- **Training**: Does your department—or entire workforce—want to improve its efficiency and effectiveness? My seminars and presentations range in length from 60-90 minutes to half-day seminars. www.LyndaMcDaniel.com/Training.asp

Topics (which are always customized to your needs):

**1. Effective Business E-mail: From Junk Mail to Special Delivery.**
www.LyndaMcDaniel.com/EffectiveEmail.asp
**2. Find Success with GPS: Grammar, Punctuation & Style.** www.LyndaMcDaniel.com/FindSuccess.asp
**3. Eureka! Jump-start your writing, creativity, and results**. www.LyndaMcDaniel.com/Jumpstart.asp
**4. Extras for Emphasis: Similes, clichés, vivid verbs, and more.** www.LyndaMcDaniel.com/Extras.asp

@ **Word 4 Word:** My blog featuring four quick writing tips per posting. www.LyndaMcDaniel.com/blog.xml

@ **Speaking**: The same topics as my seminars presented at conventions, conferences, and meetings.

@ **Association for Creative Business Writing**
www.afcbw.com

Would you like to be part of an association that bolsters your ability to write well? And helps you reach a whole new level at work? Not just a book or one-time seminar but help year round, 24/7? (Assuming, like you, someone's up at 3:00 a.m., though who knows? Members in London will be sipping their morning coffee about that time.)

Over the years, I've known a lot of people who longed for such a creative community at work. They wanted someone to bounce ideas around with. Or a group they could feel comfortable collaborating with.

And that's exactly what the **Association for Creative Business Writing (AFCBW)** offers you.

**Join now and start receiving these benefits:**

- *Words at Work: Powerful business writing delivers increased sales, improved results, and even a promotion or two.* Since you already have a copy of *Words at Work*, your membership entitles you to download an e-version so you can access all the tips, tools, and techniques from your computer.
- **In Other Words**, 24 issues of the AFCBW newsletter. It's sized just right—packed with writing tips, tools, and tests, but not too much information to absorb before the next issue rolls around.
- **Online Forum**, private, monitored 24/7 online discussion forums for asking questions, sharing ideas, and fostering creativity. Advice from experts and peers keeps your writing on target and in synch with your goals.
- **Writing with a Full Deck**, 52 cards (one delivered weekly) to help practice and perfect one writing issue a week.
- **You Said It!**, annual contest for the best creative business writing…and much more.

Join now and watch your creativity at work blossom.
www.afcbw.com

Thanks again, and I look forward to hearing from you.

Lynda McDaniel
Powerful business writing—faster, stronger, better

# Acknowledgements

Although I dedicated this book to all the editors who helped me along the way, I'd be remiss if I didn't specifically thank Hope Daniels, editor-in-chief at *AmericanStyle* magazine, who's offered me great assignments and editorial direction for almost two decades. And Anne Simpkinson, who founded one of the best magazines I've ever written for: *Common Boundary*. Her keen editorial judgments taught me a lot about storytelling. Thanks to Jonah Lehrer, who generously granted me permission to quote his work, and to the creator of *www.ImageGenerator.org,* who gave me permission to use his clever Einstein-at-the-blackboard image. Deep appreciation to Tiffany DeEtte Shafto at Contemporary Publications for her unfailing enthusiasm while designing this book. I don't know what I'd do without Virginia McCullough—writer, book editor, and friend. And heartfelt thanks to Gina Willis—proofreader, editorial coach, and best friend.

# Great Books

Goldberg, Natalie, *Writing Down the Bones,* Shambhala, 1986.

Goldstein, Norm, *The Associated Press Style Book,* Perseus Books Group, 2004.

Lamott, Anne, *Bird by Bird*, Anchor, 1995.

Lehrer, Jonah, *How We Decide*, Houghton Mifflin Co., 2009.

Manhard, Stephen J., *The Goof-Proofer*, Fireside, 1999.

Spears, Richard, *NTC's American Idioms Dictionary,* McGraw-Hill, 2000.

Strunk and White, *The Elements of Style,* Longman, 2000.

Urdang, Laurence, The *Synonym Finder,* Warner Books, 1978.

White, E.B., *Writings from the New Yorker* 1927-76, Harper Perennial, 2006.

Zinsser, William, *On Writing Well*, Collins, 2006.

# Index

# About the author

Lynda McDaniel is the director of the Association for Creative Business Writing (AFCBW), an organization designed to offer support to everyone in the business community who wants to improve his/her writing. Before launching her own writing business, Lynda worked for several businesses and found the atmosphere too often restrictive and unsupportive. A couple of decades and a successful freelance career later, she still sees that atmosphere taking its toll on employees and managers—and their results. The Association for Creative Business Writing offers an exciting alternative.

Lynda's career includes national and regional clients such as DuPont, Kennedy Center for the Performing Arts, Georgia Institute of Technology, High Museum of Art, Atlanta Convention & Visitors Bureau, and the Asheville Chamber of Commerce. She has helped hundreds of executives, managers, and employees write with confidence and style at the City of Seattle, Seattle Chamber of Commerce, U.S. Small Business Administration, University of Puget Sound, University of Washington, YMCA, Cutter & Buck, First Choice Health, and Kroll Security, as well as many one-on-one coaching clients.

Her long career as a journalist includes feature articles for magazines and newspapers such as *Law & Politics, Associations Now, Southern Living, Country Living, Yoga Journal, University of Chicago Magazine, Restaurants USA, American Cinematographer, Atlanta Journal-Constitution, Charlotte Observer, and Seattle Post-Intelligencer.* Online credits include *guideposts.com, beliefnet.com,* and *washingtonpost.com.*

Lynda wants to hear from you. She's available for one-on-one consultations as well as speaking and training engagements with your company or civic organizations. Contact her at www.LyndaMcDaniel.com or www.afcbw.com

Image courtesy of www.ImageGenerator.org